THE STEAM AGE
IN COLOUR

R Preston Hendry
&
R Powell Hendry

GUILD PUBLISHING
LONDON

This edition published 1985 by
Book Club Associates
By arrangement with
Blandford Press
Reprinted 1986
Printed in Spain by:
Printer industria gráfica s.a.
Barcelona D.L.B. 33484-1984

Plate 1: The ingredients which made up the steam age were legion, and all who knew steam at first hand will have their treasured memories, perhaps of a branch motor train, or a pacific simmering in a city terminal, an aroma of hot oil, steam and smoke enveloping the bystander, or, as here, one of those maids-of-all-work, Stanier 'Black Five', No. 44829, at the head of a parcels on the already doomed GC main line, in November 1965, a haze of steam and smoke marking her progress.

Contents

Introduction and Acknowledgments

The story which unfolds in these pages is about colour photography, and the steam age on Britain's railways, an era which stretched from the dawn of the last century to the close of the 1960s. For much of that period, the only way to record events was in monochrome, or 'Black and White', for early colour processes were slow, coarse grained and inaccurate until the late thirties. By the 1950s, there had been further dramatic improvements in colour film, but even at the close of the Steam Age, the colour photographer was in the minority, and film speeds slow compared to today. The preservation scene is nowadays lovingly recorded in colour, but such a record of the great days of steam is far rarer. For many years, the authors have dreamed of creating a portrait such as this, which would not only recall British steam, but the development of colour photography itself, depicting such long forgotten systems as the addition-screen Dufaycolor process.

In the 120 colour plates which make up this book, 80% being the work of the authors, the rest coming from originals in their collection, emphasis has naturally been placed upon the steam locomotive, 67 classes being portrayed. The railway environment also receives a long overdue mention, for the signal boxes, stations and sheds were an intrinsic part of the steam age, and the steam locomotive is best studied in its setting, not in isolation.

Many books upon steam depict British Railways, but overlook the wider spread of British steam, and we have strayed further afield to recall locomotives which once belonged to the Ulster Transport Authority, Great Northern Railway (Ireland), Sligo Leitrim & Northern Counties Railway, Coras Iompair Eireann, industry, and the narrow gauge County Donegal and Isle of Man systems. Such was the diversity of steam, that 120 views can no more than scratch the surface; one is forced to be selective, and if the reader should lament the omission of his pet class, spare a thought for the authors, who had to exercise the judgment of Paris between different 0-6-0 goods, or single and double chimney GWR *Counties*. Their inclusion would have meant an omission elsewhere.

Thanks go to the railway officers and staff of all grades who granted us facilities not always open to the public, and without whose co-operation, many views would not have been possible. A special vote of thanks goes to Mrs Elaine Hendry, both for enduring many hours of waiting, whilst her husband and son were 'on safari', and for directing her own camera upon steam from time to time. Many of the classes we have depicted are no more. In some cases, sister engines live on in preservation, and we even see a few engines, now saved for posterity, during their service lives.

LION

▲ *Plate 2: The Steam Age dawns* – Despite the pioneering role of the Stockton & Darlington Railway, the Liverpool & Manchester is commonly held to be the first fully developed public railway. L&M 57, *Lion*, built by Todd Kitson & Laird in 1838, and the oldest workable locomotive in the world, glides silently through Dunchurch station on her little known 1961 steaming. To stand on the footplate, and to fire this veteran, as one of the authors did, was a wonderful experience, for less than a decade separated *Lion* from Stephenson's *Rocket*. Truly a miraculous survival from the dawn of the steam age. Look at the magnificent polished firebox and boiler cladding, and the slender coupling rods.

Plate 3: Twilight of Steam. – BR 'Britannia' pacific No. 70031 *Byron* bursts out of the south portal of Kilsby tunnel on the Lakes Express on 7 August 1964, only months before electrification of the West Coast Main Line. At first sight, she has little in common with the *Lion*, yet steam is created and used in just the same way. The difference is in size (and in a century of design experience), not in concept, a reminder of the tradition of the steam age. As a further link, at the same time as *Lion* was taking shape at the Airedale Foundry in Leeds, the Stephensons were wrestling with the awesome problem of completing Kilsby Tunnel, one of the enduring monuments of the Railway Age.

Plate 4: Today, we can take excellent colour photographs at the touch of a button. Modern films, meters, auto-focus and exposure, and lightweight cameras, having obviated most of the work — and even skill. The photographers of 100 years ago faced a very different task. Enormous mahogany and brass cameras, large glass plate negatives with prolonged exposure times, and a deadly array of poisonous chemicals were their constant companions. To appreciate the development of colour photography, it is instructive to look at the work of one of the greatest of the pioneers, R E Bleasdale. In company with a handful of colleagues, Bleasdale created a wonderful portrait of steam in the North East, some of his views still being available from archival collections. Bleasdale himself favoured a rich 'plain chocolate' sepia, very different from the mild chocolate brown used by many contemporaries. An original 'Bleasdale' is both a rare and a prized possession. Through the medium of this book, we are able to reproduce such a view taken from a contemporary Bleasdale print.

The locomotive is a North Eastern Railway 'long boiler' 0-6-0 , No. 658. The original is so excellent that the details of the maker's plate can be read, 'No. 1747, R Stephenson & Co, Engineer, Newcastle upon Tyne, 1867'. The modern camera could do no better! The plate recalls other Bleasdale characteristics, such as the date, August 15th 1881 added upon the tender, and the crew posing with their steed, for this was long before the days when 'action' photography was practicable. In studying a selection of Bleasdales, one realises that the locomotives were often brought to the camera, one after the other, rather than the reverse. It was easier that way, and less time consuming!

Author's Collection

Chapter 1

'Steam and Colour'

The steam railway came into being to meet a definite need, that of industrialists of the early nineteenth century for a better transport system than was offered by the horse and wagon or the canals. The first railway locomotive was Richard Trevithick's Pen-y-Darren engine of 1804, built for use on an ironworks tramway in South Wales. Practical difficulties ensued, and nearly ten years elapsed until reliable engines were built for the collieries of the north east. Another decade elapsed before the completion of the Stockton & Darlington Railway in 1825. Even then, the 'true' railway was yet to be born, for the S&D was essentially an industrial railway. The first true public railway was the Liverpool & Manchester Railway, which opened in 1830. In the ensuing eighty years, more than 20,000 miles of railway were to be completed, worked at their peak by a like number of steam locomotives.

An interest in railways developed almost as soon as there *were* railways to be interested in. In part this was a fascination with the new-fangled, or the prospects of limitless wealth held out by some promoters. Nevertheless, there was a growing interest in the railway itself, directed primarily towards the steam locomotive. Many writers have sought to explain this attraction, dwelling upon the visual impact of steam, smoke, twirling rods, speed and power, or the teamwork necessary between man and machine, or even the haunting blend of permanence and change. Perhaps it is impossible to define, but one of the first fruits of this love affair between man and machine was a wish to record it in all its moods. At first, this was the sole preserve of the artist or lithographer, but the first photographic processes were announced by Daguerre and Talbot in 1839. Photography developed alongside the infant railways. Exposure times of several minutes prevailed, but gradually cameras and photographic emulsions improved. The work of one of those pioneers, R E Bleasdale is illustrated opposite in a plate prepared from a contemporary Bleasdale print. With the long exposure times, 'action' photography was far in the future, and with a dozen glass plates filling an extremely heavy box, photographers had to be sparing in their choice of subject. Early emulsions were sensitive to a narrow range of colours, and the appearance of commercial 'ortho' plates in 1882 was a major breakthrough. Almost a quarter of a century was to elapse before red-sensitive panchromatic plates became available, and this explains the glossy black appearance of early views of Midland Railway locomotives, despite their crimson lake livery.

Plate 5: Exciting though monochrome was, the desire for a colour record persisted. Whilst researchers strove to devise a colour system, practical interest turned towards blending the skills of the photographer and the artist, and the painting of monochrome photographs provided colourful scenes which were technically sound. Plate 5, depicting a Stroudley 'G' class single, No. 348 *Lullington*, outside Littlehampton shed, has been prepared using traditional techniques from a glass plate original, of this delightful engine in its LBSCR finery. *Lullington* was built in 1882, and withdrawn in 1908. The yellow ochre livery of the original (and the painting), are sensitive to lighting, only coming 'alive' in strong sunlight.

№ 772
772

▲ *Plate 6:* In the previous plate, we illustrated both the colour techniques and express power of late Victorian times in the south of England. We move forward forty years, to see a Maunsell 'King Arthur', No. 772, *Sir Percivale* on a down express at Hewish Summit, two miles west of Crewkerne, and at the start of the long racing stretch to Axminster, on the LSWR Salisbury – Exeter line. This study, taken at mid-day on 13 August 1938, is one of the few pre-war colour views of an express at speed suitable for reproduction to large format. It was taken on a 3¼ x 2 Dufaycolor transparency at 1/100 at f4.5.

THE DUFAY OUTFIT

1. Dufay Slide in Card Mount.
2. The Instruction Sheet.
3. The Filter (rolled).
4. Dufay "120" Film.
5. A Dufay "120" Carton.
6. The Slide Envelope.
7. A Modern 35mm. Slide.

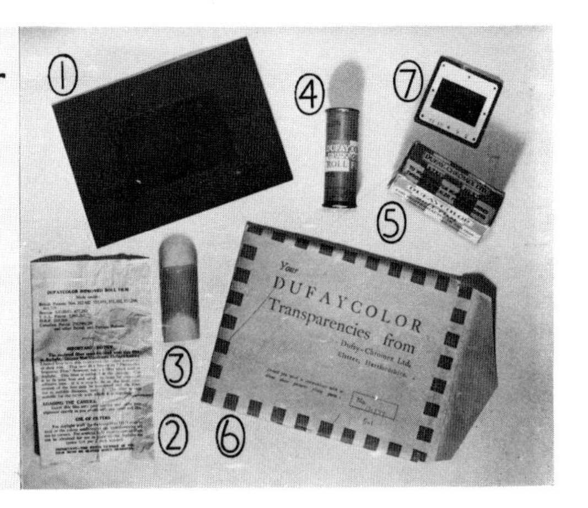

Plate 7: Few modern photographers will ever have seen the harlequin red and yellow Dufay film cartons or slide envelopes. Dufaycolor survived the war; 'Despite War Conditions, Dufay-Chromex Limited have been able to improve the colour rendering of their film'. Even so, photographers had to cut and fit a daylight filter supplied with each film to achieve correct rendition, whilst artificial light filters had to be specially ordered, quoting the film batch, due to production differences. Film speed was 10 ASA, plus or minus a stop, a coding with each film giving the necessary adjustment!

The theory of colour photography was first propounded by J Clerk Maxwell in 1855. Colour vision is the work of the cones in the human eye, which variously respond to one of the three primary colours, red, green or blue, other colours being a combination of these. Yellow, as used by artists as a primary colour, is in fact a mixed colour. In 1861, Maxwell took three monochrome plates of a ribbon through baths of red, green and blue liquids, and projected positives of the images simultaneously on a screen, using lanterns with similar 'filters'. Colour rendition was poor, due to the rudimentary emulsions, yet he had proved that by taking three monochrome views through the correct filters, and combining the three images on screen, that colour photography was feasible. A filter of one primary colour passes light of that colour, but blocks light of other colours, so where a red component is present in a scene, a positive of a red-filtered negative will be transparent, and where red light is absent it would be opaque. The same applies to green and blue. By projecting these three positives, a colour picture is created. Taking three consecutive views was a nuisance, and cameras were devised to take the three masters through their correct filters. A less cumbersome alternative was to design one filter which combined the three colours in a non overlapping pattern so fine that the human eye could not distinguish them. This is the basic idea used in the production of colour work in books and magazines. The first commercial colour 'screen' was produced in 1895 by ruling fine red, green and blue ink lines on a gelatin coated glass plate. The screen was mounted with an ortho plate in the camera, so that light passed through the screen before striking the plate. Beneath a red line, the plate only received red light. The screen was so fine that the red, green and blue images merged when viewed. The Lumiere brothers, pioneers of motion picture, devised a random screen using dyed starch grains in 1907, offering exposure times of as little as two seconds in sun. Louis Dufay improved the line screen in 1909, and with ONLY an 80% absorption of light, slashed sunlit exposures to a second. Film speeds continued to improve, and in the 1930s, roll film replaced glass plates, Lumiere switching in 1931, quickly followed by Agfa. Dufay offered roll film from 1935, and film speeds as high as 6 to 10 ASA were feasible.

Light losses in the addition process prompted research into the alternative subtraction system, where unwanted colours are eliminated, rather than red green and blue images created separately. Red light is absorbed by a filter of the other two primary colours, ie blue-green (or cyan). Green light is affected by a red-blue image (or magenta) and blue light can be regulated by a red-green image (ie yellow). Each of these complementary colours thus absorbs one primary colour, and by combining images, a colour picture is created, without the need for a screen of starch grains or ink lines. One answer was a camera with suitable internal reflectors which would take three separate negatives, which were combined for printing. Further work showed that two negatives could be taken together, a 'bipack' with the third via a reflector; by the late 1920s, 'tripacks' were available, saving the need for a special camera in subtraction work. Results were patchy, and the ideal was a single base coated with three emulsions, individually responsive to red, green and blue light, and which could be processed to yield the complementary colours of cyan, magenta and yellow. Technical problems abounded, including migration of dyes, but in 1935-36 Kodak issued cine and still film. Colours were still pastel, but rendering, definition and translucency outclassed the oft-times sombre addition screen system. Alas the dyes were not all stable, a problem which was to haunt other manufacturers later. Considerable changes had to be made in 1938. Agfa introduced a film similar in concept, but radically different in technical detail.

E. FRANCIS & SONS L

▲ *Plate 8:* A GWR 57XX Pannier tank enters Leamington Spa station bunker first with a modest freight about 1938. GW devotees will find much of interest, from the light stone and brown water column, to the indescribably grimy platform starter, and the lamp standards. This plate is prepared from a Dufaycolor transparency.

Plate 9: A domeless Stanier 5XP 'Jubilee' No. 5564 *New South Wales* heads a rake of crimson lake LMS stock towards Euston in this evocative late afternoon study of the west end of Rugby station prior to the installation of colour light signals in 1939. An engine blows off in the sidings to the left of the running lines, whilst hump shunting has been in progress on the right, the wagons in the sidings (just above the locomotive chimney) having come off the hump, which is controlled by the signal by the Abbott coke wagons. The numeral on the LMS brake van, LNWR water column, the fire devil, and fogman's hut repay study.

The appearance of the Dufay addition process, and Kodak subtraction process, made railway colour photography a feasible proposition — although only just, but with Europe plunged into total war from 1939, any photography became difficult, as the film manufacturers switched to war tasks, whilst the photgrapher was likely to attract disapproving looks, if not outright arrest, where sensitive subjects, such as railways, were concerned. When peace returned in 1945, film was in short supply, and photographers were glad of the occasional B + W film, let alone colour! The advent of a labour administration in 1945, pledged to a programme of nationalisation, presaged many drastic changes, and despite strong protests, and their outstanding war record, the 'Big Four', the Great Western, Southern, London Midland & Scottish and London & North Eastern, along with most of the surviving independents, were swallowed up into British Railways on 1 January 1948.

Plate 10: The shortage of colour film in 1945-50 was a great tragedy, for many transient liveries were lost. By reverting to Victorian techniques of blending the work of photographer and artist, we are able to recall one such scene. During the war, 935 'Austerity' 2-8-0s had been built for the Ministry of Supply. 200 of these were bought by the LNER after the war, and renumbered into LNER stock from February 1947, becoming class 07. No. 3010 heads a freight past Staverton Road on the GC London Extension in 1947. Under BR, the ex LNER 'Austerities' were assimilated into the rest of the class in a 90,000 series.

▼ *Plate 11:* The advent of BR spelled finis for many proud liveries, but heralded a whole range of new colour schemes as well, the most controversial being the blue livery adopted for a few top link express classes. The livery was discontinued in 1951, and disappeared quite quickly. No. 6016, *King Edward V*, one of the magnificent GWR 60XX 'Kings' calls at Leamington Spa with a Paddington express in 1952. The original is a rare early Ilford colour slide, using the subtraction process devised by Agfa before the War, and whose 'knowhow' became generally available after the War, in the Allied countries.

Plate 12: 'Under the Transport Act 1947, responsibility for the administration, maintenance and operation of British Railways, together with certain ancillary services, passed on 1st January 1948 to the Railway Executive, which acts as agents of the British Transport Commission . . .' Thus began the first annual report of the BTC on its largest undertaking. It WAS an immense organisation, with 20,101 locomotives less than 100 of which were diesel or electric, 19,662 route miles and 8,270 stations. Although the railways had become badly run down, due to the war, and this was one excuse used by government ministers to justify nationalisation, the real reasons were political, rather than practical. The newly formed BTC and RE faced an unenviable task, for they had inherited four proud concerns, each with its own traditions and autonomies, which, at the dictat of the politicians, THEY had to weld into some new shape. The direction, and even the degree, of that process were bound to be controversial, and even the image which was to be projected generated much heat, as old and cherished liveries were axed. Each region was accorded its own house style, but with thousands of stations, this took years. Brinklow, on the LNWR Trent Valley line, was still in faded LMS paint in 1953-4. The road collection and delivery lorries were one of the 'ancillary services' mentioned by the BTC. The RE inherited over 52,000 road freight vehicles, divided almost equally between internal combustion engine and horse-drawn. Interestingly, they received the carmine and cream livery otherwise reserved for express passenger stock, one of those delightful ironies of the early BR period.

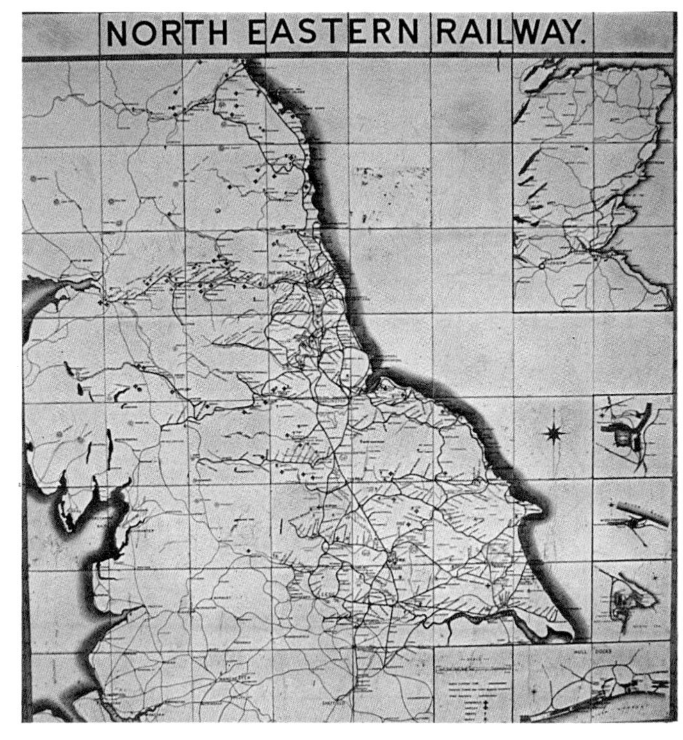

Plate 13 (Above): Each Region was accorded a distinctive colour. For some, the choice was automatic, green for the Southern, chocolate for the Western or maroon for the London Midland region. Scottish Railways were hived off from their east coast or west coast alliances to form a new Scottish Region, and the national colour of light blue was an obvious candidate. The LNER lines in England were split in two, to form the Eastern Region and the North Eastern Region. The new house colours had to be distinctive, and the ER opted for dark blue — the LNE men had a penchant for blue. With dark blue at one end, and light blue at the other end of the North Eastern region, something had to be done, so the new region selected Tangerine, possibly the most striking of all the regional house colours. Enamel station signs appeared in the new colours, as at Beverley where a venerable North Eastern Railway train shed survived to delight the connoisseur. Look at that mass of tangerine signs, set off rather nicely by the clump of Valerian on the right.

Plate 14 (Above Right): Although there was a new name on the timetables, the old order lived on, and pre-group names, as well as the big four, were cherished in many places. This magnificent North Eastern Railway tiled wall map, in NER 'colours' of pale milk chocolate, survived at Beverley, despite that awesome array of tangerine signs.

Despite the new initials and colours, the railway network inherited by the BTC was traditional in outlook, and with less than 100 diesel or electric locomotives out of 20,000, the very idea of change was unthinkable. Indeed, the RE itself was soon to underscore steam's permanence with the announcement of a range of new standard steam classes, the first of which appeared at the start of the fifties. Meanwhile, in its first annual report, the BTC revealed that the assumed useful life of its locomotives was from 30 to 50 years, according to type. The inference was clear, motive power was being built which would carry BR through to the closing years of the century. By the 1980s, the pre-group engines would have gone, as would many grouping designs, but a sizeable selection of Bulleid, Collett, Gresley, Stanier and other late grouping types would be in daily traffic alongside many thousands of BR standards. The enthusiasts of the day, though they mourned the demise of the old liveries, recorded the passing scene as the availability of film, cash and time permitted. Other than for the odd threatened species, often to be found on remote branch lines, there was no *need* for a sense of urgency. Was it not clear that engines still on the drawing board would be running for 30, 40 or 50 years to come.

Plate 16: Vehicles overhauled between 1 January 1948 and the transfer of the NCC to the UTA, bore one of the now rare 'RE NCC' plates.

Plate 15: One of the more improbable assets to be inherited by the Railway Executive in 1948 was the 203 miles of 5ft. 3in. broad gauge and 42 miles of 3ft. 0in. metals owned by the *L.M.S. Northern Counties Committee* in Ulster. The Midland Railway was to blame; in 1903, the MR had purchased the then independent Belfast & Northern Counties Railway, and this had passed to the LMSR and finally to the RE. The RE did not actually want a railway in Ulster, but the Belfast government did, and had legislation in hand to create a road and rail authority, the Ulster Transport Authority, to control all road and rail undertakings operating solely within the province. The NCC was sold to the UTA as soon as this could be arranged, the sale being backdated to 1 January 1948. The price was £2.67m, or £10,875.92 per mile. As the NCC lost a considerable sum of money each year, this was not a bad deal. Midland thinking had naturally played a part in NCC motive power policy, and when new engines had been needed in the 1930s, the Midland rear-guard at Derby seized their chance. With the Hughes-Fowler *crab*, and then the advent of Stanier, they had never been able to create an MR mixed-traffic 2-6-0. The NCC needed engines, Stanier and his men had more important things on their mind, and Derby did so want a 2-6-0 to play with. The Fowler 2-6-4T, widened to 5ft. 3in. gauge, shorn of tanks, and with a tender tagged on, fitted the bill. NCC 'Mogul' or W class No. 97, *Earl of Ulster*, shunts a GNR(I) bread van at Portadown station on 29 August 1964. Before the war, these engines had borne the full crimson lake livery, yet even in black, they show us what Midland steam power might have looked like had '1923' never taken place.

Plate 17: When the NCC required more motive power after the war, with an ability to work anything from an express to a pick up goods, the simplest answer was a 2-6-4 tank version of the Moguls. The 'WT' tanks, or *Jeeps*, as they became known, have been attributed to both Stanier and Ivatt. In fact, they are what Derby would probably have built for the Midland if left to their own devices. Ten jeeps were built for the NCC in 1946-47, and a further eight, Nos. 50-57, for the UTA in 1949-50. The first of the UTA batch, No. 50, is bathed in mellow evening sun, as she accelerates a southbound express out of Portadown on 1 September 1964.

Plate 18: Partition of Ireland in the early 1920s created a number of International railways within the British Isles. The only main line company was the Great Northern Railway (Ireland), whose 112 mile main line connected Belfast and Dublin. The GNR(I) was adding new steam power as late as 1948, including five Vs class 4-4-0s, the last 4-4-0 design ever to enter service in the British Isles, and a simple version of some 1932 Compounds. They were named after rivers, and No. 207 *Boyne*, accelerates a heavy Dublin express south from Portadown on 29 August 1964, when in the ownership of the UTA, though still bearing the azure blue express livery of the erstwhile GNR(I). Nowhere else in the British Isles could one still see 4-4-0s assigned to regular duty. Truly the last of a proud line.

Plate 19: The 43 mile Sligo, Leitrim & Northern Counties Railway, built to ship cattle from the west of Ireland to the GN, for onward transmission to Britain, was also affected by partition. It was single track and habitually penniless. After 1882, most new engines were 'long boiler' 0-6-4 tanks, the last pair being ordered just after World War II. By the time Beyer Peacock had completed them, in 1949, the SLNCR could not afford to buy them, so they were shipped to Ireland in 1951 on HP terms! With the closure of much of the GN in 1957, the SLNCR perforce had to close, and both tanks were bought by the UTA. The SLNCR did not hold with numbers, and they had been *Lough Melvin* and *Lough Erne.* The UTA retained their names, but numbered them 26 and 27. *Lough Melvin*, which had worked the last train on the SLNCR, is seen at Belfast, York Road shed, on 30 August 1964. She was withdrawn in 1965 and sold for scrap in 1968. Note the archaic long and short coupled wheelbase of the 'long boilered' engine, the firebox being behind the rear most driving wheels.

Plate 20: The coal fields of the North East were the cradle of the steam locomotive, and whilst the locomotive and the railway soon outgrew that cradle, steam power remained vital to industry. In tracing the development of steam, and of colour photography, we have once again had recourse to an early sepia portrait. With the dense network of routes in the British Isles, industrial railways rarely reached any great size, as there would be a mainline company nearby, but a few systems in the North East operated substantial mileages, and adopted main line operating methods, including tender locomotives and signalling. One of the most important was the *Earl of Durham's Railway*, based upon Philadelphia, Co Durham. With some 70 miles, and with extensive operating powers over the NER, the Earl of Durham's Railway, later to become Lambton, Hetton & Joicey Collieries Ltd, had need of main line freight power, such as No. 11, seen in the 1880s. Note the 4w chauldron wagons then in use, and which persisted in the North East for many decades thereafter.

▼*Plate 21:* In 1948, orders from industry were still flowing into the steam locomotive builders works, and Robert Stephenson & Hawthorns turned out this neat 0-6-0 saddle tank for the Rugby Portland Cement Company's New Bilton works. When this view of RPC No. 5 was taken, one sunny but icy January day, one of the authors was old enough to enjoy a footplate ride, but hardly appreciated the direct link with the Stephensons', which the burnished maker's plate, 7387 of 1948, signified.

Plate 22: F. W. Hawksworth, last C.M.E of the Great Western Railway, inherited the Churchward tradition, and whilst high degree superheat, 280lb. boiler pressure and other new ideas, such as welded tenders or continuous splashers, found their way into Western thinking, the Hawksworth *Counties*, the last design of GWR 4-6-0, were recognisably in the Swindon mould. Originally equipped with single chimneys, trials were made with double chimneys on two engines, but No. 1022 *County of Northampton* was the first to receive a production example in May 1956. She is seen at Leamington Spa a few months later, bearing the first lion and wheel emblem. None survived into preservation. The wheel tapper, and the musical ring of a sound wheel, are an enduring memory of the days before the ultra sonic tester replaced the human ear.

Chapter 2 In A Traditional World

Below Over the decades, a Great Western tradition had built up for such mundane items as labels, and whilst there might be a new 'owner' with a new name, Western men saw no reason to alter the style of their forms, or even the reference numbers. On the LMS, there was a similar spirit. Most of *their* stationery was pre-fixed with an 'E.R.O' code. The London Midland Region simply put in the new title and left it at that.

Despite the new liveries and insignia of the early BR period, it was business as usual, whether in the West Country or the Highlands, but no-where was the resistance to change in the essentials more apparent than on the Western Region, for apart from anything else, the GWR had been spared the upheavals of a new identity at the Grouping, and tradition was at its strongest. The fact that GWR engines, because of the cast numberplates, retained their old numbers and BR green was similar to GWR green, helped as well.

▼*Plate 23:* Away from the important stations, life proceeded much as it had always done. The village station master had time to chat about the potato crop or the cricket team. Fenny Compton station recalls that leisurely era. A few parcels await the next train, but passenger traffic is not expected to be heavy to judge by the pile of sleepers at the foot of the platform ramp, or the oil barrels propped with a couple of bricks. Several loose roofing slates call for attention.

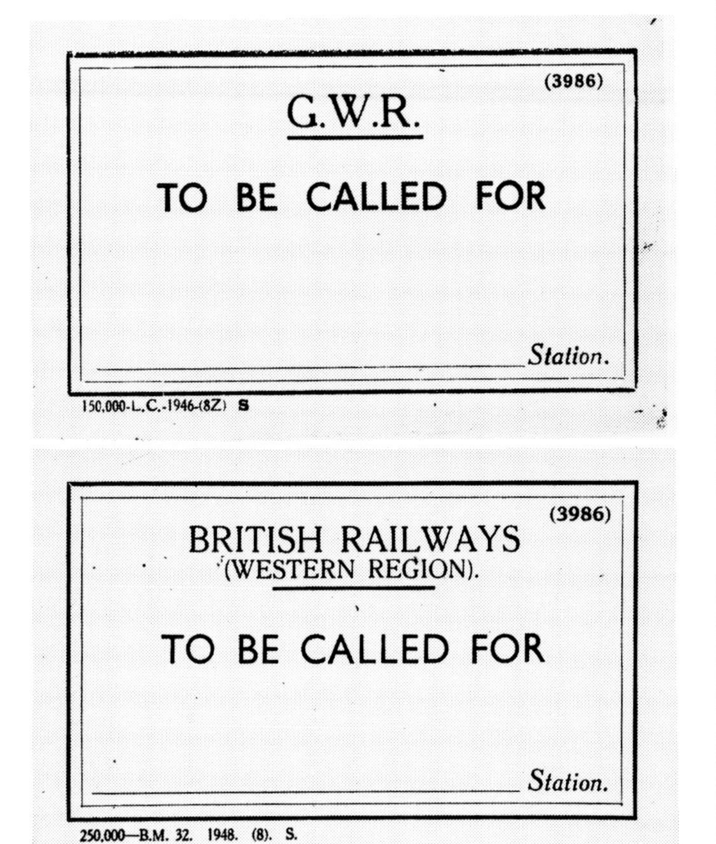

(3986)

G.W.R.

TO BE CALLED FOR

Station.

150,000-L.C.-1946-(8Z) S

(3986)

BRITISH RAILWAYS
(WESTERN REGION).

TO BE CALLED FOR

Station.

250,000—B.M. 32. 1948. (8). S.

CHESTER No 4
CHESTER
GENERAL

▲ *Plate 24:* Whether at a busy junction, or a quiet country station, the pleasing tinkle of the block bells could be heard, giving forth their mysterious codes, which the signalman, in neat uniform waistcoat and trousers, converted into a frenzy of activity, as levers clashed over, points moved and signals came on or off. To those who cared to master the intricacies of the block code, it was an open book, 4 bells — an express; 3-pause-1 pause-1, a fully fitted goods. On the London & North Western Railway, dissatisfaction with the signalling equipment available from the commercial manufacturers, prompted the redoubtable Francis William Webb into creating a complete system of signal boxes, lever frames, locking, signals, signal arms, and even block instruments. Webb is often disparagingly remembered for the alleged foibles of his compounds. A more accurate memory would be his 2-4-0 Jumbo's, Cauliflower goods, or signalling. Chester No. 4 box of 1904 was fitted with the later type of Webb frame, the tappet frame, which was more compact and permitted a low structure. The LNW gantry has 23 pressed steel arms.

Plate 25: Most enthusiasts were familiar with the exterior of the signal box. Venture inside, and one was in a fascinating world, where colour coded levers were handled with consummate ease by the signalman, who soon acquired the knack of moving heavy points or slotted signals with the minimum of effort. Signal levers were red, points — black; facing point locks — blue; distants — yellow, and spares white. The Webb frame, with its front mounted stirrup, instead of the usual rear mounted catch handle, was unique to the LNWR. North Western men swore by it; most other men simply swore at it. Nevertheless such frames lasted a century in service, and many survive yet. Preston No. 1 box is alas no more, but bathed in the warmth of the electric light, as the short January day fades into dusk, we sense the industrious, yet cosy atmosphere of a big mechanical box.

Plate 26: Beneath the lever frame, in the locking room was a world seldom visited by anyone outside the signal department. Here, the heavy interlocking, which is the vital part of the ensemble, is housed, and, in the days before the micro chip, steel and brass were fashioned into a kind of movable jigsaw, to prevent conflicting routes, and potentially dangerous moves, being set up by a moment of error up above. We see an early 'tumbler' locking frame at Lancaster No. 4 box, another giant LNWR cabin on the West Coast main line, which survived into the age of electronics, but is now no more. The interlocking of very large boxes required deep locking racks and high structures. Had Chester No. 4 been so fitted, it would have been an extra storey tall!

Plate 27: It is difficult even today to assess the BR *Standards*, due to the controversy which surrounded their birth, career and demise. They were announced as a balanced range which would ultimately permit the hundreds of existing classes to be whittled down to a few, with concomitant savings in spares. The change from established company traditions was resented by many railwaymen and enthusiasts, whilst the adoption of almost transatlantic lines, to improve accessibility, was controversial. Their teething troubles were magnified, and when dieselisation began, the very concept was lampooned, a criticism given bite by the abrupt cessation of construction, and their brief careers. No. 73000, class leader of the 172 Class 5 4-6-0s built from 1951, seen in glorious weather at Banbury on 30 October 1965, typifies the breed.

Plate 28: Part of the design philosophy behind the 'Standards' was to provide a range of efficient modern locomotives of varied axleloads and power output to meet all needs. The 76¼ ton Class 5 4-6-0s were therefore complemented by the 69 ton Class 4 engines, with a greater route availability, and which were seen as replacements for a whole plethora of pre-group 4-4-0s and 4-6-0s. No. 75008, drifting through Oxford tender first on a transfer trip, demonstrates the value of the cut away tender and rear spectacle plate fitted to certain BR standards. Were the standards an unnecessary switch from company designs, and an unattractive anachronism, or the final flowering of British steam, their careers marred by events which are more apparent with hindsight than at the time? There have been many answers to that question; no doubt there will be many to come.

Plate 29: The Ministry of Supply 'Austerity' 2-8-0s were devised to meet an emergency. Simplicity of construction, economy of material, and ease of maintenance took preference. They were rugged, unlovely machines. BR inherited 200 from the LNER, whilst others entered stock from government ownership, until 733 bore BR insignia. Other members of the class were to be found in Holland, Sweden, Hong Kong, and even on the Longmoor Military Railway. Their designer, Robin Riddles, became first CME of BR, and in these gaunt machines can be seen the design philosophy, with somewhat greater concession to looks, which shaped the BR Standards. Simplicity of construction and ease of operation are the criteria by which they have to be judged, and this portrait of No. 90730, at Barrow Hill shed, Chesterfield, on 24 July 1964, stained as she is by rust and boiler sediment, shows that working conditions had not improved. Alas no BR example was preserved, but a former Swedish engine runs on the Keighley & Worth Valley Railway.

The early part of the BR era witnessed the end of many company traditions, but the nature of the railway itself was not threatened. The Railway Executive was steam orientated, and foresaw an end to arrears of maintenance, a railway worked by more modern and more efficient steam locomotives, but life otherwise scarcely altered. There were a few main line diesels, including the LMS pioneers 10,000 and 10,001, whilst it had been accepted that the diesel shunter would be the logical replacement for the 0-6-0 tank, on account of the long periods of idleness of most shunters. The GWR had considerable experience of diesel railcars, while the LMS NCC, despite its small size, had a good deal of practical knowledge as well, which was available to BR. To suggest that steam was under threat was absurd, although worrying developments across the Atlantic showed what the diesel lobby were capable of. A change of government, at the start of the Fifties, inevitably led to a new Transport Act in 1953. After less than 6 years, the whole railway establishment was re-organised. The RE was abolished, control of BR passing directly to the Railway Executive's former overlord, the British Transport Commission. As a necessary corollary, the powers of the regions were strengthened, and a greater measure of autonomy allowed. Political pressure was exerted upon the BTC to be 'progressive', which being translated, meant doing something, though 'what' remained vague. The BTC, having criticised its RE for its traditional approach, was both vulnerable and receptive to such counsel, and a top level re-organisation and re-think occupied much of 1954. The Commission's 15 year modernisation plan was published in January 1955. Instead of the £600m needed to maintain the status quo, the BTC sought £1,240m, to provide new marshalling yards and freight stock, better passenger facilities and carriages, and extensive dieselisation and electrification. 1955-1957 was to be a period of preparation, 1958-59 of development and 1960 onwards of achievement. Steam construction would end, but it was expected that there would be a substantial 'rump' of steam operation at the close of the period.

Plate 30: The first tangible signs of the re-organisation were the adoption of regional carriage liveries, the Western seizing the chance to return to happier memories! No. W13074, a BR-built Mark I Corridor First, bears a proud livery, and a proud headboard, reminding us that Paddington – Birmingham – Birkenhead was once a major express route.

Plate 31: The London Midland Region predictably felt that maroon was the only reasonable colour to apply to carriages, and set to work with a will to banish the carmine and cream, which, despite all the rude remarks levelled at it during its life time and subsequently, had more to commend it than many liveries. By this time, colour emulsions had made further progress, and with improved definition and speed, it became possible to record dramatic combinations such as steam at speed in the snow. No. 46127 *Old Contemptibles* roars south past Hillmorton Sidings at the head of the up Emerald Isle Express shortly after noon on 8 January 1959. This plate, taken from a 35mm Kodachrome, was close to the limits of photographic emulsions, for whilst the snow reproduced excellently, the darker colours of the stock received barely enough direct sun and reflected light to expose at a reasonable speed. As the majority of cameras only opened up to F3.5 or F4, instead of the F2 common today, the problem was compounded. This illustration was in fact taken on an F3.5 Zeiss. Single lens reflex cameras, with inter-changeable lenses, and ultra sophisticated in-built metering were virtually unheard of.

Plate 32: No. 7020 *Gloucester Castle*, sporting the second BR lion and wheel emblem, leans into the curve, as she powers a Birmingham express through Southam Road & Harbury Station in 1963, bringing a moment of life and vigour to an otherwise peaceful scene, with the GWR Italianate buildings little altered from Brunel's day. Appearances were deceptive, for a hidden terror lurked within the harmless-looking corrugated-iron oil and general store visible on the extreme right, a menace unearthed by one of the authors, when invited by the station clerk to browse for old GW forms, prior to a 'clear out'. Apart from oil, paraffin and stationery, the hut contained a cardboard box; the box contained detonators. The GWR rule book prescribed that detonators were to be returned to store 'when bearing any signs of rust on the outside of the case'. The detonators in that box — a large one — bore little sign of anything *but* rust. The moral here is — beware of GWR corrugated iron huts. This study was prepared from a 35mm Agfacolor slide. No. 7020 was one of the BR built GWR Castle class, and had she enjoyed the intended lifespan of these locomotives, would have been active until the early to mid eighties. The Southern and Western Regions made considerable headway with their regional coaching stock colours, but LM maroon was adopted as a standard, and *in this WR scene,* the stock is all in maroon.

Plate 33: From the earliest days, the railways had consciously applied the principle of cross subsidisation, meeting the deficits on their most lightly used branch lines from surpluses elsewhere. Between the wars, there had been some pruning of the most unremunerative services, but the railway network passed to nationalisation largely intact. For a time, petrol rationing provided an artificial protection to the railway, whilst a high level of military traffic, due to National Service, was a further stimulus. The end of petrol rationing at the start of the fifties, and the build up of private motoring, forced a re-appraisal in a number of cases. These included the picturesque Bromyard – Leominster branch in Herefordshire. This closed to regular passenger services on 15 September 1952. In those days, abandonment tended to be protracted, and parts of the route were used for wagon storage for quite a while, but with retrenchment in the air, lifting was decided upon. The S.L.S. organised a farewell trip from Worcester on 26 April 1958, which is depicted in Leominster station. The locomotive, No. 4571, one of the earlier 'straight tank' 45XX small prairies, was one of the few members of that class to carry lined green livery AND the early BR lion and wheel emblem, for the switch from black to this more lively scheme had only recently been made, and the early emblem was soon to be superseded. GW devotees may recall that this was the first new locomotive upon which that distinguished railway historian, the late H M Le Fleming worked, during his period with a GWR erecting shop gang at Swindon.

Plate 34: By the fifties, BR was starting to feel the pinch, as costs steadily mounted, and traffic fell away in the face of road competition. In Ireland, where there was a much smaller 'cake', the strain was far worse, and by 1953, the proud Great Northern, despite its busy Belfast – Dublin route, was on its knees. Complete closure was averted by joint action by the Belfast and Dublin governments, who funded a Joint Board until the railway was partitioned in 1958, after drastic closures. Surviving lines in the south went to the CIE, whilst the UTA took over routes in the 'Six Counties'. Motive power was similarly divided. GNR (I) No. 174 *Carrantuohill*, an S class 4-4-0, was one of 5 sisters built by Beyer Peacock in 1913. Owing to the parlous state of the Boyne viaduct, they had extra light frames, but in the 1930s, both bridge and locomotives were rebuilt. No. 174 passed to the CIE in 1958, but with the end of CIE steam in 1963, faced an uncertain future. In the north, UTA steam was badly run down, and four engines, including No. 174 were sold to the UTA as a stopgap. The S class were at home on every duty from pick up goods to crack express, and it is on the former that No. 174 is seen at Strabane on 1 September 1964, still bearing her GN lettering, the last engine to do so in regular service in Ireland.

Plate 35: Another line to struggle against all the odds was the County Donegal Railways Joint Committee, which, like the GNR (I), achieved 'International' status at the partition. The 'Donegal', owned from 1906 by GNR (I) and the Midland Railway, served the wilds of West Donegal from a railhead with the GN at Strabane. For its passenger services, the Donegal was a pioneer of petrol and diesel railcars, but steam was retained for summer excursion work and freight traffic. Relentless economy staved off closure until 31 December 1959. The CDRJC, with 124 route miles of 3ft. 0in. track and severe gradients, was the largest 'NG' system in the British Isles, and required powerful locomotives. These included five 'Class 5' tanks of 1907, built by Nasmyth Wilson at a cost of £2475 each. Originally numbered 16-20, they were re-numbered and renamed in 1937, upon the demise of older stock. No. 16 *Donegal* became No. 4 *Meenglas*. She is seen at Strabane, the junction with the GN.

Plate 36: The 'Donegal' operated a total of 59 carriages, all but the first 11 being bogie stock. With the growth of railcar working from the 1920s, many were broken up, or converted to freight stock, but more than twenty were retained into the 1950s for excursion traffic. CDRJC No. 30, a 'corridor third', or in normal parlance a saloon, was built by Oldbury in 1901. The absence of numerous heavy internal partitions meant that No. 30, and a sister vehicle, were no heavier than the average 6-wheeler, and much lighter than the bogie stock. No. 30 was pressed into service as a light-weight trailer, to operate with the more powerful bogie railcars, of which the CDRJC possessed several. Roller bearings were fitted to ease the task still further, and proved invaluable. She too is depicted at Strabane. Thanks to the Midland Railway, the BTC gained a 50% stake in this most unlikely outpost of empire, and unlike the NCC, this was not sold off. In 1948 the book value of the BTC share was placed at almost £½m.

County Donegal Railways Joint Committee.

"Section Clear, but Station or Junction Blocked."

CAUTION TICKET.

No.__________Issued at__________

For__________Train to__________

NOTICE TO THE ENGINE DRIVER.

The Section is clear to__________

but you may expect to find the Signals there at

DANGER.

____

SIGNATURE.

Date__________

[OVER.

Plate 37: During the fifites, an increasing number of branch closures, coupled with the spread of the DMU, reduced the scope for the traditional branch line tank. Quite modern classes, such as the Collett 0-4-2Ts of the Great Western were prematurely put into store, or withdrawn from service. The branch motor train had been an institution for decades, and the demise of these pretty little engines was a great blow to enthusiasts. No. 1444, a Collett 14XX is on shed at Westbury in 1964, by which time the steam branch had all but vanished. The 14XX, originally 48XX, had been built to replace the 517 class 0-4-2 tanks of Victorian times, and were one of several instances of the GWR providing a modern version of an early design. The weathering details on the bunker and truck should be of interest to the modeller.

Chapter 3

The Pace Quickens

Until 1954, BR had turned in a modest profit each year, so the politicians were relatively peaceful. In 1955, the year the Plan was unveiled, BR barely made ends meet, and in 1956, a loss of £16.5m was recorded. The problems associated with the operation of a largely traditional railway now asserted themselves in the form of political pressure to do something. The BTC was again vulnerable, having criticised the RE over its old fashioned approach, and then having declared steam to be obsolescent. One of the main planks of the modernisation plan was that steam was uneconomic; if steam *was* to go, saving the taxpayer a fortune, as promised in the package, then the sooner the job was done the better. America was conveniently held up as a glowing example of rapid dieselisation, though it was generally forgotten that the Electro-Motive-Division of General Motors, the power house of the transformation, had many years of diesel traction experience prior to the avalanche of orders. Nobody in Britain had that experience, but it was assumed that UK manufacturers would be able to adapt their considerable road transport, marine and stationary engine experience to rail work, for future orders, export business and their reputations were at stake.

At first, the Modernisation Plan was a distant cloud, rather than an imminent threat. Steam construction was to cease, but in the official mind it was clear that there would be a sizeable 'rump' of steam operating into the seventies, and perhaps beyond, if the Standards which were rolling out of the various works were to enjoy a reasonable service life. There was still a lot of water to flow under the bridge — or more appositely, to be boiled! When the modernisation plan appeared at the start of 1955, there were 18,420 steam locomotives in stock, as against 391 diesels and electrics. New construction, of 174 steam locomotives, many being powerful main line types, outstripped the 136 diesels acquired, mostly shunters. Indeed, some of the benefits of the modernisation plan could hardly be gainsaid; diesel shunters and DMUs, however lacking in charm, did offer savings compared to steam, and with deteriorating financial returns, adherence to the old order might simply precipitate crisis and closure. Much of the technology was already proven for these vehicles. The main line dieselisation plan was a cautious one, with 174 prototype diesels to be tested thoroughly, to gain experience of a wide range of transmissions, engines and other details. After the trial period, decisions could be taken upon which types to multiply. BR information handouts for the press emphasised the long term nature of the plans 'Up to the present, British Railways have relied on the steam locomotive as the main method of traction, and although steam locomotives will still be used in some areas, they are in the future to be largely superseded by diesel or electric traction'.

The fragmentation of BR into six semi-autonomous regions fuelled the flames, for now that steam had been labelled old-fashioned and extravagant, each region bid fiercely for its fair share, and more, of the annual diesel cake, citing its own special needs. Despite misgivings within the BTC itself, the cake expanded, acquiring a mind of its own. During 1956, the DMU fleet mushroomed, from 179 vehicles to 453; 1000 were expected to be delivered in 1957 and 1200 in 1958. At least that technology was proven. For main line diesels, it was a different matter. Pressure was now being exerted to order in production quantities, in some cases prior to the prototypes entering service, let alone proving their worth. By 1959, reality bore little resemblance to the cautious plan of 1955. The BTC carried out a re-appraisal 'By spending more in these years, the intention was to reap the benefits earlier'. Realistically, they might have added that the strategy had gone out of the window, in the hope that tactics would win not just the battle, but the war.

Whatever the regrets of the steam diehards, change was inevitable, for steam was both costly to operate, and owing to its inherently dirty nature, with many arduous jobs, it was becoming increasingly difficult to recruit staff for such work. The initial modernisation plan could well have led to a tidy and ordered move to greater efficiency, whatever its emotional implications. The tragedy of the fifties was that the politicians had created a situation where steam was not the only casualty; common sense and caution were equally old fashioned.

Plate 38: Despite the Plan, there was still room for optimism, and in 1955 ten of the new BR 9F 2-10-0 standards were completed with Crosti pre-heating boilers beneath their ordinary boiler, in an attempt to wring greater efficiency from the steam locomotive. The Crosti system had shewn considerable economies when applied to elderly Italian steam locomotives, but with a modern and thermally far superior design, the savings were not regarded as sufficient to justify the added complications and costs. After a trial period, the Crosti pre-heaters were sealed off. It was a brave try, and one regrets that the device was not applied to some of the older classes, where savings comparable to Italian results might have been expected. The *Crosti's* spent much of their life heading coal drags along the Midland main line, but No. 92028 is caught at Rugby, a London Midland Region 'Western Lines' shed, in August 1964. The Crosti pre-heater did not improve the looks of the 9F 2-10-0s, but had it been applied to older engines, as would have been the more logical, its effect on appearance would have been bizarre to judge by Italian experience. The Crosti boiler, Giesel ejector, and advanced compounding on the Chapelon principle, must remain some of the 'ifs' of the steam age, though with steam in 'disgrace', it is doubtful whether any degree of improvement could have turned the tide.

Plate 39: One of the standard 9Fs, No. 92091, one of a block of engines allocated to Annesley, wheels a fast freight southbound through Rugby Central on the GC on 12 September 1964. Details of the sand drag should appeal to the modeller, as this is a feature one seldom sees reproduced.

Magnificent though the 9Fs were, they heralded the end of an era. In 1955 BR had added 174 new steam locomotives to stock. In 1960, the total was three, all of them 9Fs. The last was No. 92220 *Evening Star*. Steam construction had ended.

Plate 40: The Crosti boiler represented the most fundamental attempt to improve the efficiency of the steam locomotive, but BR continued research work for a number of years, with the final paradox that just as much of the inspired — or at times, un-inspired — guesswork on steam design was resolved, construction came to an end. This story of gradual development of new or existing classes is exemplified in the Gresley pacifics of the LNER. Gresley was an early advocate of superheating, and his first A1 pacific of 1922 was an advanced locomotive for its day. The 1925 interchange trials against the GWR *Castles* showed hitherto unexpected flaws, and Gresley was wise enough to accept the lessons, and introduce his A3 class from the late 1920s. The importance of good steam passages and draughting were not lost to Gresley, and numerous experiments were carried out, and these were continued by BR, culminating in the fitting of double chimneys to many engines, including A3 pacific, No. 60100 *Spearmint*, portrayed at Carlisle Kingmoor in June 1964. The softer exhaust of the modified engines offered useful benefits, but worsened a long-standing problem, smoke obscuring the drivers vision. Innumerable smoke lifting devices had been tried between the wars, and by BR, and on the A3 pacifics, extensive use was made of the German-inspired Trough deflectors. The ungainly double chimney and deflectors hardly added to the looks of No. 60100, but were at least a positive attempt to improve performance.

Plate 41: As we have seen, an interest in railways developed as soon as there were any railways, but a popular mass appeal was far in the future. In the 1930s, organised shed visits became more frequent, and the process resumed after the war. With the withdrawal of many older types, nostalgia for the pre-grouping era became more widespread, and with it, an awareness that there was a potential 'market' to cater for. Primarily this was developed by the pioneer private preservationists, of the Talyllyn and Festiniog lines, but the Scottish Region displayed a commendable willingness to promote such business. The Region had inherited two preserved historic locomotives from the LMS, the legendary Caledonian Railway single, No. 123, and the epoch making Jones Goods No. 103; to these two engines, both of which were put back into working order in pre-group liveries, the Scottish Region added a pair of ex LNER 4-4-0s, *Gordon Highlander* from the Great North of Scotland Railway, and *Glen Douglas* from the North British. 'Caley' No. 123, the doyen of the quartet, is at Carlisle Kingmoor.

Plate 42: As well as depicting the Caledonian 'crest', an audacious appropriation of the national heraldry of Scotland by a proud company, which, in the minds of many travellers, came to represent Scotland, this portrait also recalls the eye catching light blue livery adopted by the CR. The makers plate, Neilson & Co Glasgow 1886, tells us a little of the history of this celebrated machine and of Scottish engineering. Neilson was one of the great Glasgow locomotive builders, and turned No. 123 out just prior to the Edinburgh Exhibition of 1886, where she was on display. After the show, No. 123 entered Caledonian service, and earned immortal glory during the 1888 Railway Race to the North. Surviving into LMS ownership, she became No. 14010, and upon withdrawal in 1935, was set aside for preservation. She was returned to active service by the Scottish Region in 1958, and the wanderings of the Scottish quartet, along with the equally celebrated *City of Truro*, from 1957, must have stimulated interest in railways. Directly, or indirectly, some of the readers of this book may owe their interest in railways to just a handful of Victorian or Edwardian steam locomotives.

Plate 43: Llanfair PG is celebrated on account of its fearsome name, yet the station had an equal claim to merit as a survivor into the age of colour film of an archaic form of station layout. The pioneers used wagon or coach turn tables where later engineers used points; this permitted short but squat station layouts, which relied extensively on horse or manual shunting. By the 1870s, longer layouts, suitable for locomotive shunting, were in vogue, and the old layouts disappeared. Occasionally, physical or other obstacles prevented the acquisition of the necessary land, and an old configuration survived, as at Llanfair, depicted at the start of the 1960s.

Plate 44: Llanfair's better known claim to fame was its 58 letter name, for which the LM region provided the requisite enamel station nameboard. This *was* slightly longer than average, and was manufactured in three sections, and required five posts to support it. British Railways provided a literal translation. A looser, but intelligible version would be 'The Church of St Mary, in a hollow of white hazel near to a rapid whirlpool, and to St Tysilio church near a red cave'. Clearly no-one was taking any chances with a vague description of the locality.

Although most enthusiasts kept their cameras pointed firmly towards the steam locomotive, the railway environment as a whole had much to offer. The railway station itself, so often nothing more than the backdrop to a photograph, was frequently a mine of information, and merited study. Indeed, it is fair to say that the locomotive was invariably the most modern, and perhaps the most standardised object appearing in many such views. For those who took the time to seek, a story would often unfold before one's eyes, which could be supplemented by more formal research.

Apart from the remarkable name, for which giant platform tickets were issued, and the archaic goods yard, Llanfair possessed many other points of interest. In plate 43, of the station and yard, we can see the extensive provision made for side and end loading facilities. In the days when the Chester & Holyhead Railway was built, Llanfair being the first station in Anglesey, road surfaces were very poor, and the only effective alternative to rail transport was the canal, which was restricted as to the areas it could serve. The great majority of long distance journeys soon came to be made by rail, whether of passengers or freight. The wealthiest of the passengers sometimes wished to take their own road carriage with them, and end loading facilities sprouted at even the most humble wayside stations, for this was an era when the gentry had a major voice, and it was frequently their voices and drive which brought the railways into being, or on occasion thwarted them. Side loading facilities were appreciated by the farmer for his cattle, by the gentry for their carriage horses and 'hunters'. In due course, horse drawn removals vans traversed the country on rails, providing one of the first door to door services.

Just a few yards away was the faithful old yard crane with its shaped wooden jib and long handles for the station staff to turn. In LNW days, Llanfair had a 1½ ton crane, later upped to 5 tons, quite a sizeable load for a minor wayside station. A pair of cattle wagons are in the road next to the platform.

The station buildings date from LNWR times, and replaced a cramped and squalid Chester & Holyhead original. The story is told that one LNWR District Engineer, Hedworth Lee, had regularly sought improvements to his section but to no avail. One night, he was awakened with the news that Llanfair was on fire. Gleefully he replied 'Let it burn'. A new station was duly provided.

Plate 45: From the first organised excursions in the 1840s, the railway's involvement in the holiday business, in mass terms, a development of Victorian times, grew to immense proportions. The premier holiday centres were the seaside resorts, and facilities at places such as Llandudno, Southport or Scarborough were determined not by the needs of the resident population, but to cater for the myriads of visitors who would cram a succession of trains on long hot summer Saturdays. No. 45531, *Sir Frederick Harrison*, named after a former general manager of the LNWR, and one of the last *Patriots*, nears Southport Chapel St with a summer express on 22 July 1964. These engines, often known as Baby Scots, originated in a massive rebuild of some of the Bowen Cooke *Claughton* 4-6-0s of the LNWR. In fact, little remained of the original engine, and in later members of the class, even the fiction of a rebuild was discarded. Although many carried the names of their LNW 'ancestor', even the nameplates were new!

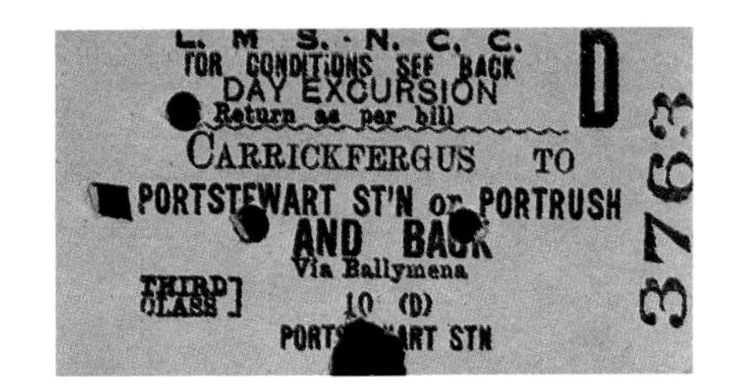

Holiday resorts, such as Southport, differed greatly from one another, yet at the same time, they had much in common. The traffic was intensive, but was confined to the summer months, particularly July and August, and was at its peak on Saturdays, as works and other holidays were commonly on a 'Saturday to Saturday' basis. Many boarding houses were geared to this, and would not even quote for mid-week business. The immense strain which such concentrated traffic imposed on the station can hardly be exaggerated. Generous carriage stabling was a must, and in plate 45, row after row of carriages can be seen in the roads in the left hand distance. More stock sidings sprouted on the right hand side of the running lines, which are from Manchester and Preston. There was also an electrified route from Liverpool, and the third rail of the extension of this service out to Crossens is visible in plate 45. Adequate platform accommodation was often a problem, and at Southport, this was solved by the construction of the London Street Excursion platforms on the left hand side of the view. No canopies were provided, as they were for summer use only, and platform facilities were kept to a minimum, but long broad platforms with few obstacles were ideally suited to handle the massive crowds. On the skyline, beyond the LMS 2-6-4T is the capacious water tank and coaling stage of the steam shed, whilst to the right of this is St Luke's signal box, an elevated box carried on girders, and an early example of power working, built by the Lancashire & Yorkshire Railway. This box, and a second power box at Chapel St station itself were needed to cope with the Summer Saturday rush. Here alas, was the Achilles' heel of the traffic. Locomotives, carriages, stations, platforms, sidings, were all geared to cope with a few Saturdays each year. Whilst costs were low, and old stock could be used, it was viable, but the Saturday crush was to fall a victim to rationalisation, just as steam itself.

Plate 46: In Ulster, the summer Saturday exodus from Belfast was just as hectic. From Queen's Quay station, the Belfast & County Down Railway dispatched train after train of venerable six-wheelers; at Great Victoria St, the GNR (I), sent out more modern stock behind innumerable 4-4-0s; at York Road, headquarters of the LMS NCC, they sent the people to Portrush, or Larne or Whitehead, part way out on the Larne line, where they even built an excursion station. North of Whitehead, the Larne line was single track, worked by electric train tablet equipment, to avoid the possibility of two trains entering a single line section from opposite directions. The signalmen were in communication by means of a combined block instrument and electric 'staff' machine, and only one token could be withdrawn from the instrument. The signalman would then put the token into a pouch with a large hoop, and it would either be picked up by the engineman manually, as in this case with NCC Jeep No. 6, or by means of an automatic exchanger. No. 6 was one of the LMS built members of the class, and this traditional scene was photographed at Whitehead as late as 25 August 1966.

Plate 47: At running sheds throughout the British Isles another scene was equally familiar, whether in the mellow light of a glorious summer evening, or the chill winds of mid winter. Enginemen would book on duty in the early evening, and check over their steed for the night's work, a slow moving freight locomotive, to head one of the long distance night goods which carried the country's merchandise north, south, east and west. This particular scene is at Portadown on the Great Northern Railway (Ireland) — it could just as well be anywhere. The locomotive is a GNR(I) SG3 0-6-0, renumbered 33 by the Ulster Transport Authority. A similar engine pokes out of the roundhouse on the right. The roundhouse table is in the foreground. On the left, partially obscured by steam and smoke, is a more modern class UG goods. A pile of clinker and ash lies at the foot of the water tank.

▼ *Plate 48:* A few minutes later, as the evening shadows lengthen, No. 33 pours a column of greasy black smoke into the evening sky as her fireman readies her for the night goods to Omagh. Pressure is well up. In the distance, another column of smoke tells of yet another 0-6-0 at work. The date is 1 September 1964. Such scenes would have been commonplace a century previously; soon they will end.

UT
N 176

Plate 49: The 0-6-0 was a versatile machine; on some railways it needed to be! No-where was this better shewn than on the Great Southern & Western Railway, whose 119 examples of the '101' class acted as shunters, freight engines, bankers, pilot engines, and even handled race or pilgrimage specials. The first was built in 1866; the last in 1903. At the turn of the century, the GS&WR had 178 engines all told. They served through Great Southern days, and to the end of steam on Coras Iompair Eireann in the mid sixties. No. 151 was built in 1868, is seen on an Irish Railway Record Society trip on 18 March 1963, and after a spell on occasional service for sugar beet specials, was withdrawn in 1965, by which time regular steam on CIE had ended.

▼*Plate 50:* The steam worked Groudle Glen Railway in the Isle of Man was another casualty of the early sixties. Opened in 1896, as a pioneer 'pleasure railway' in the lovely Groudle Glen, this short line possessed two locomotives, *Sea Lion* of 1896, and the slightly larger *Polar Bear* of 1905. The line ran from a Swiss Chalet station in the glen out on to a headland, and was cut back after the war, only *Polar Bear* remaining in use. By the end of the 1950s, she was ailing, and despite a bright 'fairground' livery for 1961, the end came when her boiler was too far gone at the end of the 1962 season. She is seen at the post-war terminus in August 1961. Happily she survives at the Chalk Pits Museum, Amberley. Look at the roofed toastrack coaches.

Plate 51: By the early sixties, steam was in retreat on BR, on the UTA and CIE; except on the preserved lines or in industry, narrow gauge steam was a memory in England, whilst the closure of the County Donegal on 31 December 1959 wrote an end to Irish narrow gauge steam. The 3ft. 0in. gauge Isle of Man Railway was run by an extremely forceful and able man, Allan Mylchreest Sheard. Manager from 1927 (and appointed at the height of a bus war), Sheard's Indian red liveried Beyer Peacock 2-4-0 tanks rolled out of Douglas for Port Erin, Peel and Ramsey. Until the early sixties, an all year service survived, but Sheard finally bowed to the inevitable and made the Ramsey line 'summer only'. No. 8 *Fenella* of 1894, and the last of the original small boilered engines in traffic, heads the first train of the 1963 season through Ballaugh on 3 June 1963.

Plate 52: The nerve centre of Sheard's system was Douglas station. We have a signalman's view of No. 13 *Kissack* of 1910 shunting in the goods yard on 19 August 1965. Two long platforms projected out from the concourse and booking offices, that on the left being for Peel and Ramsey trains, and on the right for Port Erin services. Arrivals were at the inner faces of the two platforms, engines escaping via a central release road. Coaling was from wicker or wire mesh baskets by the two water columns in the centre of the station, for turn-round times of as little as ten minutes were common during the high season. For those who regarded the narrow gauge as a quiet backwater, 12, 14 or 16 coach trains, double headed or banked, carrying a thousand passengers, were quite a surprise, yet that is what the railway was laid out to do. The golden domes of the entrance on the skyline on the left are just that – covered in gold leaf. One of the company's red painted delivery lorries, a 1940s Morris, is visible in the yard, as is a rake of wagons, one conveying bottled gas. 'AM', as he was known, had died in office just a few weeks previous to this view.

Chapter 4

Western Steam Finale

The Western Region entered the Sixties with a variety of steam power, but the traditions bequeathed by Churchward, Collett and the other great men of Western steam were under increasing threat, for the Western Region had embarked upon a substantial dieselisation programme, using the Warship, Western and Hymek diesel hydraulics. Diesel shunters were displacing the ubiquitous pannier tanks, whilst the DMU, or branch line closures, had eroded the place of the host of suburban and branch tanks from the pretty little 14XX 0-4-2 tanks to the high stepping 61XX prairies. To the enthusiasts of the day, a new urgency was dawning. In the late forties, steam would last forever, or for 30-50 years at least; by the mid-fifties, large areas of the country would be dieselised by the early seventies. By the early sixties, it had narrowed to the next few years. It was difficult to say when. Some classes, such as the Kings or the Castles, acquired a cult following, and as the magazines were opened each month, one scanned the withdrawals pages hoping *not* to find news of particular favourites. All too frequently, one did. Inconceivable though it may now seem, in this day when any steam locomotive is nigh-on worshipped, less significant classes could still perform their duties largely un-heralded. One of the authors was then at school, and in company with like-minded school friends, paid regular visits to the GW Birmingham main line at Southam Road and Harbury station, a wayside station with a small goods yard and a neat little signal box. A 'probable' Castle working was awaited with baited breath. In the distance would come the sound of an engine working hard, and then round the corner the train would come into view. Sometimes it was a Castle; on other occasions the result was different. 'It's only a Hall' would come the cry, and a line of cameras would go down, though fortunately not that of the author — he didn't reckon he had enough Halls yet; — *he still doesn't*! In a year's time, a mere Hall was a very welcome sight on a train; then they were all gone, sitting in forlorn rows on shed, or awaiting the breaker's torch. Only a Hall indeed!

▼ *Plate 53:* 'A mere Hall'. The cameras do NOT go up as a Hawksworth 'Modified Hall' heads a freight southbound through Southam Road and Harbury station on 12 September 1964. *Mere Hall* in this case was quite correct, for such was the name bestowed upon No. 7915 when she left Swindon works in 1950. The author apologises for the inconveniently placed post, but the plate was the result of a sprint along the far platform, up the footbridge steps, across the bridge itself, and a hurried check on exposure and focus; it is what our American cousins would call a 'grab shot', but we could not resist a mere Hall passing by, with no one else even grabbing it! Although beautifully clean, and still bearing her smokebox and cab numberplates, No. 7915 has lost her nameplates, a situation all too common in the closing years of Western steam, with plates removed by BR as a precaution, or by an element amongst enthusiasts. Indeed stories were rife of 'a friend of a friend of someone one knew' who had slipped the crew of an engine 'a fiver', and had returned home bearing a weighty trophy. How much reliance could be placed upon such stories is open to doubt, but an element of pilfering undoubtedly went on. For those not inclined towards such activities, the alternative was to buy a number plate or name plate. The authors may perhaps be permitted a story against themselves. One of the 'Only a Hall' fraternity did indeed buy a plate direct from Swindon. It cost £15, a ridiculous price, and one which would hardly last once the euphoria evaporated. It didn't; the price *went up* a lot.

Looking back through the columns of the various 'mags' is a voyage of nostalgia. The withdrawals columns include details of old half forgotten friends, and one recalls the list of survivors one all but memorised. Nos. 5000, 5002, 5014, 5018 — thus ran the list of active GWR Castles at one time. The *mere* Hall attitude explains another anomaly which puzzles a newer generation of enthusiasts — how was it that every GWR 'County' went to the breakers, or that the two Barton Wright 0-4-4 tanks, withdrawn in the early 1900s, but retained as stationary boilers at Blackpool until the 1960s were allowed to pass into oblivion. What would we give for an LYR 0-4-4T today? Nobody was very concerned about the 'Counties'; they were GWR, but not the same thoroughbreds as the Castles or Kings, and had it not been for the Barry scrapyard precious few of *those* classes would exist! As for Barton Wright of the LYR, few enthusiasts knew or cared. It was only as the sands of time ran out, that a better understanding arose, only it was too late for so many classes. Thus it was for the sailing ship or the paddle steamer as well, for such creations are often only appreciated at the eleventh hour or even later.

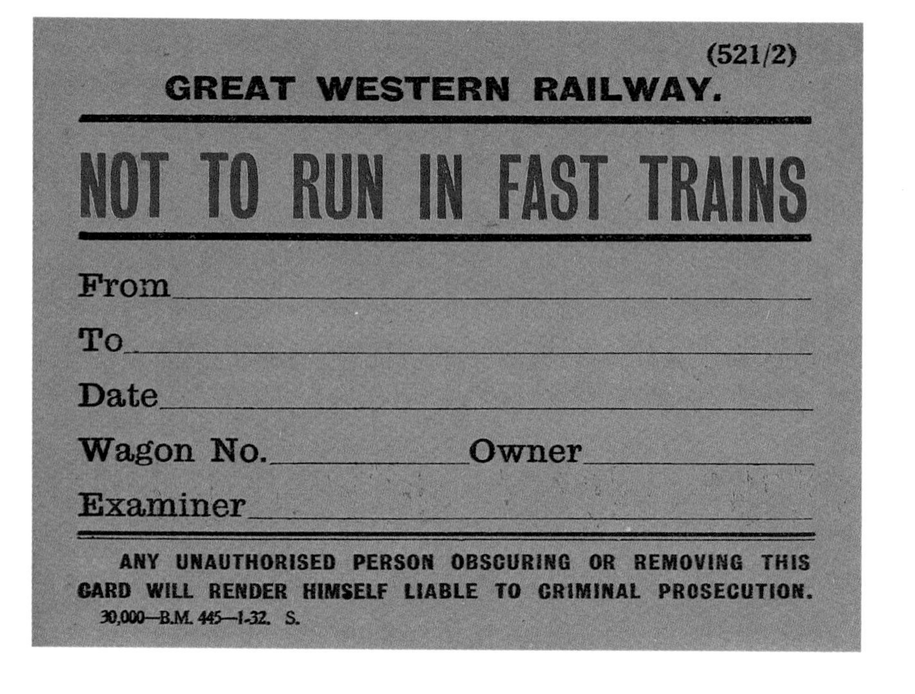

(521/2)

GREAT WESTERN RAILWAY.

NOT TO RUN IN FAST TRAINS

From ____________

To ____________

Date ____________

Wagon No. ____________ Owner ____________

Examiner ____________

ANY UNAUTHORISED PERSON OBSCURING OR REMOVING THIS CARD WILL RENDER HIMSELF LIABLE TO CRIMINAL PROSECUTION.

30,000—B.M. 445—1-32. S.

Plate 54: Nationalisation enabled Western steam to spread beyond the bounds of the GWR, with the result that seven 94XX Panniers, Nos. 8400-8406 found themselves in that Midland stronghold, Bromsgrove, for work on the notorious 1 in 37 Lickey incline. No. 8405, nearing the summit at Blackwell on 31 July 1964, was built by Bagnall in 1949, and succumbed in September 1964. The battered fire iron slung across the lamp brackets would be a worthy addition to any model. The 4 wheel vans as tail traffic at the rear of the passenger train are another source of nostalgia.

Plate 55: When the GWR absorbed the Welsh valleys line at the grouping, it found the 0-6-2T firmly in command on these savagely graded routes. Although this was not a standard GW wheel arrangement, a Swindon version was agreed, and the 56XX came into the world in 1924. Most went to the valleys; a few arrived at Leamington Spa, on the basis that the station was in a hollow with heavy pulls up towards Birmingham or Banbury. No. 6671, built by Armstrong Whitworth in 1928 to alleviate unemployment, heads a southbound shunting freight, the lowest form of life, through Harbury station in September 1964.

Plate 56: No survey of British steam should omit those ubiquitous little workhorses, the 57XX pannier tanks. So useful did they become, that with 863 examples, they were one of the most numerous British steam classes. They also managed to defeat the GWR locomotive classification system, with its curious emphasis upon the second digit. Allowing for occupied X7XX series, Swindon had to encroach into the X6XX range after a decade of construction. No. 9654 was a late example, from 1946, and is drifting through the platforms at Oxford on 8 July 1964. A DMU in the distance, still in the original green livery with V flashes will appeal to the diesel fans. At the time, it merely imparted a note of menace. No. 9654 was withdrawn that October. GW platform trollies had many uses; sometimes railway staff were inconsiderate and wanted to load mail bags on to them. More often, they provided a convenient seat for spotters, which is what the trolley by the Oxford sign is doing. Oxford shed lay just to the north of the station and one could be sure of engines running to or from shed, making a few minutes at the station well worthwhile.

Plate 57: In the closing months of Western steam, as engines ran in ever greater grime and squalor, Oxford shed evinced a last flowering of affection for its old friends, and a dash of white paint on the smokebox door and hinges worked wonders. No. 6849 *Walton Grange* is caught on shed at Banbury on 30 October 1965 in the dying weeks of Western steam. Although she has lost her nameplates, the shed staff have kept a close eye on her number plates which are still in situ, which was becoming increasingly unusual by that stage. She was one of just three *Granges* to last to the end of WR steam that December. The omission of the 68XX, or Grange class is one of the saddest gaps in the range of preserved steam, for they were real 'enginemen's engines'.

6129
PASSENGERS MUST
NOT CROSS THE LINE
EXCEPT BY MEANS
OF THE SUBWAY

Plate 58 (Above): The GWR prairie tanks had a long pedigree, going back to the original experimental Churchward 2-6-2T, No. 99. The 61XX were modelled upon the 5101 Collett series, but with a higher, 225lb. boiler pressure for London suburban work. From their inception in the thirties, they became a common sight around Paddington. Dieselisation in the late fifties and early sixties boded ill for these fine machines, but the 61XX were resilient, venturing further afield, Oxford becoming one of their strongholds. Oxford's No. 6129, in unlined green livery with the second BR crest, pauses in her shunting duties between the end of the platform and the bridge over the quaintly named Sheepwash Channel, which, for the uninitiated, connected the Thames with the Isis, just to the north of the station, and made the access to the steam shed on foot somewhat reminiscent of a railway Venice. Apart from the access, and the locomotives, Oxford shed merited interest on account of the improbability of it surviving from one visit to the next, or even for the durtion of the visit. An estate agent trying to sell it, might well have used the description 'in need of trifling repairs'.

Plate 59 (Right Upper): When the authors first spied No. 6134 tucked away at the end of a long row of other locomotives on Oxford shed one day in October 1965, she looked like any other bedraggled prairie, but as they drew closer, it became clear that No. 6134 was very special indeed.

Plate 60 (Right Lower): Though it is 30 October 1965, with the end of Western steam imminent, No. 6134 transports us back to the heyday of these engines, for upon her flank is the GWR roundel of 1934, last applied in 1942, gleaming through the mists of time, its golden hues brought vividly to life by the setting sun. The glistening roundel, a last manifestation of an old love, is made all the more poignant by the grimy condition of the rest of the locomotive, and of the early BR Lion and Wheel. The text books give excellent accounts of the liveries carried by BR steam; unlined black, lined black, unlined green and so on, yet in the latter days, steam took on a whole range of hues, not even describable, let alone described. The preservationists have created a valuable record of locomotive liveries — perhaps for completeness, we ought to have one engine in BR Improved Engine Grime, for a finish such as this was not a matter of hours or days, but years of conscientious effort.

Plate 61: 'An Abbey in the Temple'. As the end drew near, the faithful paid homage to those mighty temples to steam, the roundhouses at Oxley and Tyseley. The low winter sun filtering through the grimed windows of Oxley shed on 31 October 1964 paints No. 5089 *Westminster Abbey* in surrealist colours of gold and black, as she awaits attention she may never receive. No. 5089 was one of 16 Churchward *Stars* to be rebuilt as *Castle* class 4-6-0s. Named an 'Abbey', she was born a 'Star' and died a 'Castle'. When withdrawn in November 1964, No. 5089 was the last Churchward express locomotive, albeit rebuilt, in ordinary service.

Plate 62: The 78XX Manor 4-6-0s first appeared in 1938, and were intended as a replacement for the 43XX 2-6-0s, early examples using some parts ex the 43XX. The class spent much of its career in Wales, where they were to be found on the Cambrian Coast Express as late as 1965. No. 7808 *Cookham Manor* was purchased for preservation after her withdrawal in December 1965, and restored to GWR livery. In a dramatic action study, she darkens the skies in the deep cutting just south of Harbury tunnel on a Great Western Society special on 17 September 1966, prior to the much resented ban on steam imposed by BR after the end of ordinary steam.

Chapter 5

The L.M.S. Heritage

The London Midland & Scottish Railway was not an easy alliance of friends, or even the massive dominance of one tradition over all others, but a shotgun wedding dictated by the Railways Act 1921. It was one of the earliest results of political meddling with transport, and could reasonably have served as a warning for the future, for it was a case in which the two dominant partners, the London & North Western Railway and the Midland did not merely dislike one another; they positively loathed one another. Instead of making solid progress, the first decade of the company's history was bedevilled with internecine feuds. Had the LNWR and Midland remained separate, there would have been some friction, as had long been the case, but the politicians, by forcing them together, made a minor problem into a major difficulty.

980

Midland Railway Company.

Secretary's Office,
Derby.

The North Western, Midland and West Scottish Group Amalgamation Scheme, 1922.

Dear Sir (or Madam),

Adverting to Clause 14 of this Scheme, the Conversion of the Stocks having resulted in a fraction of Stock becoming due to you, a cheque for the cash value of the same is appended hereto.

Yours faithfully,
W. N. BANCROFT,
Secretary.

Cheque No 89921
Dated 26 Mch 1923
for 7/11 recd 27/3/23

Many stories have been recounted of this deep division within the LMS, but one reminiscence quoted to the authors by a one time LNWR fireman typifies the period. At large stations, LNW firemen were accustomed to uncoupling their own locomotives. On the Midland, this was done by station staff in many places. With the grouping, many motive power outposts, where one company maintained a small allocation in 'enemy' territory, were dispensed with, and working merged with the links from the dominant shed. This was common sense, but resulted in Midland or LNW men working into enemy territory. On one occasion, the young fireman, ultimately to reach top link duties, including the Royal Train, arrived at Leicester Midland station on a train over the MR branch from Rugby. He swung down from the cab, quickly unhooked, and was about to rejoin the engine, when he was apprehended by a livid Midland man, who informed him in forceful terms as to the magnitude of his crime, and provided a graphic description of the grievous bodily harm which would accompany any repetition. It was not merely the case that a job was at stake, but a cherished Midland tradition was under assault from the enemy!

Eventually, an LMS identity was hammered out, although old loyalties ran deep. The LMS was a remarkable railway, yet this was *despite* the efforts of the politicians, not because of them. Any rational scheme would have accepted the folly of mixing the LNWR and Midland in the same 'pot', and as the LMS was rather larger than ideal, might have encompassed a fifth group, embracing perhaps the Midland, Glasgow & South Western and the Great Central, which would have been as well inside such a setting as within the LNER.

Plate 63: At the Grouping, George Hughes of the Lancashire & Yorkshire became CME of the LMS, with Henry Fowler of the Midland remaining a powerful factor. The LMS badly needed a mixed traffic 2-6-0, which took shape under Hughes guidance at Horwich, the design being dominated by LYR thinking, as might be expected. The strains which existed lower down the ladder reached through to the upper echelons, and Hughes retired in 1925. Fowler took over, and whilst the design was too far advanced to start all over again, the Midland influence was now in the ascendant, and MR features were grafted on where possible. The most obvious evidence of this duality was the tender, which was a standard Midland design, and was much narrower than the LYR inspired cab. The Hughes-Fowler 'crab', as the new design was nicknamed, always looked as if it had borrowed someone else's tender. 245 of these locomotives were built between 1926 and 1932. No. 42900 is blowing off vigorously as she eases a rake of container wagons and 4-w vans over the brow of the Lickey incline at Blackwell on 26 July 1963. The smokebox door, with its peripheral securing clips, was a feature of early LMS motive power design, and had appeared on the Royal Scots when originally built as well. It did not survive the Stanier rebuilding with tapered boiler, so its continuance on the *crabs*, which were little altered in their 40 year career, was welcome.

As a result of this uneasy legacy of hostility, LMS motive power design displayed a number of violent changes of direction, so that there is no underlying theme, as was the case on the GWR or LNER under Gresley. The mixture of forces, with a brief period of Lancashire & Yorkshire supremacy, followed by a Midland period, which included many decidedly 'unMidland' locomotives, provides an intriguing chapter in railway history. Add to that an equally dramatic move away from the traditions of Crewe or Derby to the powerful influences of the Swindon school of locomotive engineering, tapering into a genuine LMS philosophy, and the story is complete.

42900

FORD
44431

The question 'which was Britain's most numerous steam class' is not as simple as one might think, and is influenced by whether one 'allows' locomotives which were built for war service, and which operated briefly, if at all, in the UK, and the lattitude allowed for design changes. The oldest contender is the Ramsbottom DX goods, of which the LNWR had 857, while the LYR acquired 86, or 943 in all. If the criterion were under common ownership, then the 863 GWR 57XX edges ahead. The Stanier *Black Five* mustered 842 examples, but included engines with Stephenson or Caprotti motion, which the purists may disallow. On the other hand, the BR 73000 4-6-0 was so closely based upon the Staniers, that the 172 examples might be added, giving 1014 related 4-6-0s. The 852 Stanier 8F 2-8-0s just beat the Black Fives, and there were few differences, but many were built for war service, and only 666 came into BR ownership. 935 Riddles 'Austerity' 2-8-0s were built; 733 entered BR stock, many remaining overseas. Finally we come to the Johnson 0-6-0 of the Midland and its derivatives. 865 of these class 2 goods were built for the MR, plus 10 for the SDJR and 16 for the M&GN Joint, or 891 in all. Deeley added 70 with a large boiler, the class 3 goods. Many class 2s were later rebuilt to class 3, so that the MR owned 935 interchangeable class 2/3 goods, the SDJR and M&GN engines taking the score to 961. Although class 2/3 engines were not rebuilt to class 4, the latter were no more than a large boilered derivative. With the differences in the Stanier engines, MR devotees may claim to aggregate the 961 class 2/3 and 772 class 4, to yield 1733 similar machines. GW followers will observe that this includes three boiler types, two driving wheel diameters and three cylinder sizes. Taking far less lattitude, *they* could add 240 of the '1813', '1854' and '2721' class tanks to their 57XX, making 1103 in all. With 'Cousins and aunts' . . .!

▲*Plate 64:* Although several of the constituents had long used eight coupled freight classes, the Midland had embraced the small engine policy, using 0-6-0 goods in pairs if need be. As Midland thinking dominated the LMS during the Fowler era, the Fowler MR class 4 of 1911 became the standard LMS freight engine. Despite the introduction of Fowler 0-8-0s, the Beyer Garratts, and finally the Stanier 2-8-0s, construction continued until 1941, by which time there were 575 LMS-built examples, 5 ex the Somerset & Dorset, and 192 from the Midland, or 772 in all, making them one of the most numerous classes to operate in the British Isles. No. 44431 was built at Derby in 1927, and is drifting through Manchester Victoria on 17 July 1964. She has a leaking tender, and the rear most tender axle box cover is missing. She was withdrawn later that year.

Plate 65: How it all began; in the days before effective colour film, a Midland & Great Northern Johnson class 2 goods, No. 63 simmers on shed at Yarmouth Beach station in 1928. She had hardly altered from Victorian times, and makes an interesting contrast with the Fowler engine illustrated opposite.

Plate 66: Another Johnson class which was to influence L.M.S. thinking was his celebrated 1F 0-6-0 tank, the first of which appeared in 1874, only a year after his appointment to head the Midland locomotive department. It was a straight forward 0-6-0 side tank with an open cab and a round topped firebox. 280 were built by the Midland, all but one surviving into LMS ownership in 1923. From 1919, the Midland rebuilt many with Belpaire fireboxes, whilst enclosed cabs were also fitted in many cases. 95 survived into BR days, and owing to a quirk of fate, which necessitated their retention through an agreement made a century previously, five were still in stock on 1 January 1966, Nos. 41708, 41734, 41763, 41804 and 41835. By this date the agreement was honoured by their existing, rather than doing any work. On 24 July 1964, however, when No. 41708 was photographed in Barrow Hill shed, near Chesterfield, they were still receiving maintenance, and a sister engine, No. 41844 can be seen on the sheer legs on the left. Although fitted with Belpaire boiler, No. 41708 still has her open cab, a legacy of Victorian times. When photographed, she was the oldest locomotive in operating stock, dating from 1880. After her withdrawal, she was purchased for preservation. In common with the Great Western Railway, the Midland was one of the few companies to make extensive use of the round house, compared to the straight shed favoured by most British companies. The Midland sheds were invariably much older and smaller than their GWR counterparts, and Barrow Hill could barely take an 0-6-0 tender engine in the clear on many of its roads.

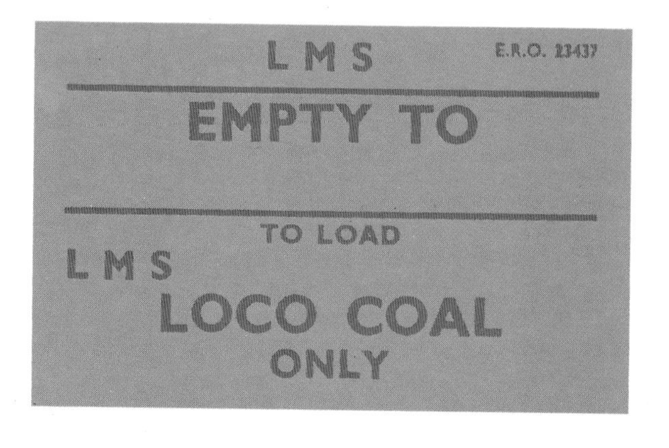

Plate 67: The Johnson 1F tank gave way to a more powerful version, the 3F tank, with larger cylinders and higher boiler pressure from 1899, and sixty of these were constructed by 1902. With 340 powerful shunting tanks, the Midland had little need of further construction, and no further engines were added until the grouping. The LMS had inherited a varied fleet of engines, and to cut down on classes and spare parts, built 415 for its own use and 7 for the S&DJR. They were provided with Belpaire boilers from the outset, but in other respects differed little from their Midland counterparts. The nickname by which the LMS engines are known to most enthusiasts, a *Jinty*, was never universal in railway usage. Indeed in some areas, a *Dobbin* was the preferred version, and the term *Jinty* would engender uncomprehending looks! *Jinty* or *Dobbin*, No. 47578, an Agecroft engine, shunts a mineral wagon in a typical industrial environment north of Pendleton on the old Lancashire & Yorkshire on 16 July 1964. The tall chimney, for Thoms Castile Soap, and nearby industrial premises, recall the surroundings in which these engines often worked.

THOMS CAS ILE SOAP

BICC
ELECTRIFICATION
42958

▲*Plate 68:* With the exception of the Royal Scots, the first fifty of which were built in haste by NBL in Glasgow for the LMS, the twenties were a period of marking time, with Midland designs which had been adequate in pre-war days being turned out as group standards, but little progress anywhere. When Sir Henry Fowler left office in 1931, E H J Lemon was to occupy the seat for a brief inter-regnum, whilst the LMS took stock, and decided upon a new direction. The existing locomotive fleet was very varied, with many elderly locomotives in need of early replacement. With the exception of the *Royal Scots* and the similar but slightly smaller *Patriot* 4-6-0s, the company had no modern passenger classes capable of handling heavy expresses to demanding schedules. The Beyer Garratts, introduced on the Midland divisions had been disappointing, due to Beyer's hands being tied by the inclusion of Midland features unsuited to this type of engine. As Midland rule had not provided the answer, and was resented by the LNW side, and LNW rule would be an equal anathema to the Midland, the choice fell upon William Stanier of the Great Western Railway. Stanier did not adhere slavishly to GWR ideas, but blended the best of Swindon with the good points of Crewe and Derby. Ten 0-4-4 tanks appeared early in the Stanier regime, but were in reality a hangover from the old era. Amongst the earliest true 'Staniers' were the 40 mixed traffic moguls turned out from Crewe in 1933-34. For the first time, the LMS enginemen experienced Swindon ideas, such as the taper boiler. The Stanier moguls lived in the shadow of later more celebrated classes, such as the Jubilees, Black Fives or Duchesses, or of older classes, such as the Crabs. They were too modern to be interesting, too mundane to be exciting, and just too numerous to be rarities. In an era which could offer the comment 'Only a Hall', what chance had an anonymous mogul? No. 42958 basks in the July sun outside Rugby shed in 1964.

Plate 'D1': — Lest steam fans complain, we have numbered this plate in the diesel series, for it does feature 'the enemy'. The story, however, is worth telling. By 1962, steam was being displaced at an ever increasing pace by diesel traction. It was all very sad. One day, the authors paid a visit to Rugby station. In due course, there was a long hiatus in London bound services. Finally, a grimy class 5, No. 44771 drew into the platform, seemingly piloting an English Electric Type 4, D218 *Carmania*. No. 44771 quickly 'dumped' her would-be successor in a siding, 'where she belongs' as someone intoned, and took the train on to Euston. To the passengers, it must have been an infuriating delay. To the enthusiast, such moments, when discredited steam had to come to the aid of its much vaunted successor, were sweet nectar. Then, even the most mundane steam engine assumed the aura of the most prestigious pacific. Even a Hall would have been worshipped! Visible to the left of No. D218 is the LMSR 1930s mechanical coaling plant. Similar structures were provided at many important steam sheds throughout the LMS, and reduced 'on shed' times and labour costs considerably. It is sad that really advanced steam handling techniques were never explored in the UK, and that mechanical coaling plants, self cleaning smokeboxes and other improvements were peripheral, rather than carried out on a large scale at selected depots to assess overall results.

Plate 69: Overleaf, we mentioned the Stanier *Black Five*, which was built in large numbers from 1934 until 1951. In plate 1, we saw a *Black Five* in charge of a parcels train. The engine in our previous view had been on pilot duty when it was called upon to cope with a failed diesel, and then take an express on to London. Here we see the Class 5 in yet another role, heading a local passenger train on the former Great Central London Extension. Although the GC was laid out as a main line, it had a local character as well, and some highly individual 'turns'. One such working was the 7.40am. ex Nottingham Victoria, which provided a suburban commuter service to Leicester Central, arriving at 8.17am. The train carried on south, expiring at Rugby Central at 8.55am, which was too late for anyone to get to work or school, as the station was in a largely residential area. Passenger traffic was not exactly heavy. No. 44984 has just arrived with the 8.55am at Rugby on 16 August 1966. The locomotive is already carrying the light engine headcode, for in a few moments, the crew will shunt their three coach rake into the down side of the station, where they will lie until 5.20pm when they will return north. The engine will run on light to Banbury shed, whence it will return in the afternoon. In less than a month, the GC was to close as a through route. No. 44984 was a regular 'central' engine, and was withdrawn that same year.

Plate 70: The uniformity of the *Black Fives* was broken by experimental modifications carried out to some 70 engines built in 1947-51. The most radical change in appearance was to the engines fitted with Caprotti valve gear, twenty having an archaic-looking low running plate with separate splashers, and two a very high running plate. They were to be found on the Midland and Western divisions of the LMR, often in nice big clumps, one early haunt being the Birmingham — Bristol line. Latterly, several congregated at Southport shed, wherein No. 44745 is seen at rest on 22 July 1964. The rust staining and marking left by water impurities should appeal to the 'weathered engine' school of modellers!

Plate 71: The modest loading gauge and train lengths imposed upon Britain's railways, partly through their pioneering role, and in part because of the philosophy of a frequent service of trains of medium length, meant that really massive displays of head end power were infrequent, in marked contrast to the States and other parts of the world, in the days of steam. Double headed 4-6-0s were about the most one encountered, or very rarely, a 4-6-0 piloting a Pacific. Just once, one of the authors encountered something far more dramatic, and it was by pure chance. Some railway friends had called in for a chat, and as it was a glorious afternoon, the author mooted the idea of an hour or two by the lineside. The others had left their cameras at home, but in the end a compromise was reached, half an hour, and no more. 'Well, of course,there won't be anything worth taking' was the general opinion. Three hundred plus tons of steam locomotive, with a combined tractive effort of 72,150lbs., was the outcome as No. 46238 *City of Carlisle* and No. 70004 *William Shakespeare* pound north through Rugby Midland station on the down fast line at the head of the Camden – Carlisle fully fitted express freight on 9 July 1964. A few months later, it was all history. No. 46238 was one of 38 *Coronation* class pacifics built from 1937 for the West Coast Main Line, and had originally been streamlined. What splendid machines they were in their LMR Maroon paint, and what a vindication of the LMS board in their decision to appoint Stanier to the post back in 1932. No. 70004, *William Shakespeare*, as Southern fans will recall, spent her early years on the Southern Region, working the celebrated *Golden Arrow*, one of the few BR pacifics to appear on that region. By the early sixties, she had migrated to Willesden and the WCML.

Plate 72: A locomotive engineer is invariably remembered for his express locomotives, even though freight used to be the backbone of the railways. When Stanier came to the LMS, freight offered as many problems as the passenger side, with just two post group classes, the Fowler 7F 0-8-0s, disparagingly nicknamed *Austin Sevens*, and the 33 Garratts, both of which were hampered by the grafting of Midland 'small engine' ideas on to large and powerful machines. As with other CMEs, Stanier opted for a 2-8-0, the first of which appeared in 1935. No. 48016 was a 1937 engine, and after requisition saw war service, before being returned to its peace time job. One of the authors was at the regulator as she was photographed drifting off Banbury turntable on 19 September 1965, acutely aware of the shed masters wrath if 120 plus tons of steam locomotive ran amok. It is entirely co-incidental that the engine was withdrawn later that year.

Plate 73: Stanier's successor, Charles Fairburn, had only a brief period in wartime to leave his mark on LMS steam, but contributed a further chapter to the LMS 2-6-4 tank story, which had commenced with some parallel boiler Fowler engines in 1927. They were intended to replace a heterogenous collection of pre-group tank and tender engines on suburban, local passenger and pilot duties. Stanier introduced taper boiler versions in the thirties, and Fairburn made further refinements, reducing the wheelbase slightly, providing larger cylinders and a slightly greater tractive effort, but reduced overall weight. 277 were built between 1945 and 1951, the last examples, including No. 42103 at Brighton in 1950-51. The sediment dribbling down from the smokebox, and pattern of grime, would keep the modeller up to scratch.

Chapter 6

The Eastern Scene

Plate 74: In preparing a portrait of the former LNER lines in England, we could not resist this enchanting study of East Holmes signal box and the adjoining Brayford Swing Bridge, less than ¼ mile from Lincoln station. The GN had a deft touch where signal box design was concerned, and the Eastern Region was happy to vary the colours, providing an eye catching white box to reflect in the tranquil waters.

Plate 75: As befitted the climate and conditions of its territory, the North Eastern Railway emanated an atmosphere of rugged reliability. As the LNER did not have the funds to indulge in wide spread modernisation, for passenger classes, let alone freight, a sizeable fleet of NER 0-6-0 and 0-8-0 freight locomotives lasted into BR days. Large boilers, commodious cabs, and a minimum of ornament characterised these ponderous machines, used to slogging along on heavy mineral drags. No. 63344, a Raven Q6 0-8-0 of 1913, was still in traffic at Neville Hill, Leeds, in March 1966, by which time many parts of the country were without steam.

Plate 76: Nigel Gresley of the GNR became the first CME of the LNER upon its formation, a post he was to hold until his death in 1941. Denied the funds to embark upon a modernisation of the sort essayed by the LMS, Gresley used his limited resources to improve performance at the top end of the spectrum, adding a range of impressive classes which kept the LNER name well to the fore. For the first decade of the grouping, his A1 and A3 pacifics stole the show, but Gresley felt that more could be extracted from the design, and for still higher speeds, opted for increased boiler pressure and other modest developments. Streamlining was one of the changes decided upon, and whilst this would reduce wind resistance at high speed, the publicity value was at least as valuable to a company as starved of funds as the LNER. A study of the vital statistics of the earlier Gresley pacifics with the new A4 class, shews how little the basic format needed to be altered, yet the figures alone fail utterly to reveal the dramatic new shape of steam. The first locomotives appeared in a striking silver-grey scheme, but later deliveries were in Garter Blue. No. 60007, *Sir Nigel Gresley* was withdrawn by BR in February 1966, but purchased for preservation, returning to the blue livery. Prior to the 'Steam Ban', consequent upon the demise of BR steam, she made a number of runs as LNER No. 4498. At this period, she was still carrying BR electrification warning flashes, whilst the front numerals were too small. Both of these features have been long since dealt with, giving this study a nostalgia appeal.

Plate 77: By the 1930s, the 2-6-0 or 4-6-0 had become the accepted types for mixed traffic work, depending upon power output required. Gresley never allowed standardisation or othodoxy to stand in the way of progress, and when the need arose for a powerful and fast mixed traffic engine, he was ready to forsake the 4-6-0, as adopted by the GWR, Southern and LMS, for a radically different answer, the V2 2-6-2. This permitted a wide firebox and improved design, and still allowed space for a good front end layout. 184 Gresley V2s were built, the only large scale use of this wheel arrangement in the British Isles for tender locomotives. No. 60966 approaches Chaloner's Whin Junction, just south of York, with a rake of petrol tankers in May 1963. The marshalling of barrier wagons between the locomotive and wagons containing inflammable or explosive substances was common.

Plate 78: One of the fascinating side effects of the run down of steam was the occasional appearance of classes in un-expected locations. One such move was the transfer of five Peppercorn A1 pacifics to Neville Hill shed, Leeds, in July 1963 for the Newcastle, and Settle – Carlisle services. The A1 design was commenced by Gresley's successor, Edward Thompson, but completed after his retirement, by Arthur Peppercorn, last CME of the LNER. 49 engines were built in 1948-49. The reign of the A1 at Neville Hill was all too brief, and they were withdrawn en masse in October 1965. From left to right, we see No. 60118 *Archibald Sturrock,* No. 60131 *Osprey* and the roller bearing equipped No. 60154 *Bon Accord,* lined up awaiting their fate at Neville Hill. Such sights had become all too common, as the pace to oblivion quickened. None have survived into preservation, so this was truly good-bye. Many readers will have poignant memories of their own last sight of favourite classes.

Plate 79: The Scottish railways developed a markedly different character to their 'sassenach' neighbours, and despite grouping and nationalisation, this remained to the fore. In part, it was due to a largely independent locomotive, civil engineering and operating tradition, and in part due to financial constraints. Operating north and west from its headquarters in Aberdeen was the smallest of the Scottish companies, the Great North of Scotland Railway. Aberdonians have long had a reputation for hard headed frugality. At Boat of Kintore, the signal box seems to have been rebuilt at some time, with a different base and superstructure, whilst the gates are an object lesson in the minimum use of expensive timber members. Even the diamond board saves the useless off-cuts which the customary circle produces! Economical in the use of material, the GNS men were generous in courtesy and assistance, as the authors gladly recall.

Chapter 7

North of the Border

Plate 80: Scottish locomotive engineering pursued an independent course from the dawn of railways through to the grouping of 1923, when the Scottish school was effectively extinguished. By the fifties, native Scottish steam was ageing, and great inroads had been made. Sharp curves and lightly laid track on many colliery and industrial spurs, and even in goods yards, necessitated a sizeable fleet of diminutive 0-4-0 tanks on the Caledonian, North British and Glasgow & South Western systems. Dumb buffers, sometimes updated with enormous sprung buffers, as in this instance, abounded, as did open back cabs, saddle tanks and grossly inadequate coal space. This was countered by providing venerable four wheel wagons as combined tenders and shunters trucks. No. 56031 was one of 39 0-4-0 saddle tanks designed by Dugald Drummond for the Caley, and built 1878-1908. She is seen at Motherwell on 26 June 1960, looking the worse for wear. All had gone by 1962.

Plate 81: In plate 79, we visited the north east of Scotland; we now turn to the south west, and the most southerly station in Scotland, Whithorn, on the Portpatrick & Wigtownshire Joint Railway. The P&W started as an independent line, but was taken over by the Glasgow & South Western, the Caledonian, the LNWR and the Midland. The Whithorn branch closed to passengers in September 1950, but remained open to freight until October 1964. An enthusiasts special, headed by a 'Caley' Drummond *Jumbo* 0-6-0 goods, No. 57375, visited the station in 1963. The similarity between these buildings and Kintore is striking, despite their differing origins.

Plate 82: Since construction began in January 1883, the Forth Bridge has become one of the best known engineering works in Britain, if not the whole world. No one view could recall the grandeur of Scotland's railways more succinctly, though ironically, the Forth Bridge was the property of three English companies, the GNR, NER and Midland, as well as the North British. Two steam trains are upon the bridge in this July 1962 study, taken from one of the passenger and car ferries which plied the Forth prior to the construction of the modern road bridge.

▼*Plate 83:* Statistics abound about the bridge; the main columns of the cantilevers rise 341 feet above high water mark; the cantilevers stretch out 680 feet and are connected by suspended spans 350 feet in length. By contrast, such meagre details as are given of the approach spans make us regard them as the merest of culverts, and in plate 82 we see why: *Here*, we see a 150 ton Gresley A3 dwarfed by this minor appendage to the bridge proper! Lynx eyed LNER fans may have identified No. 60097 *Humorist*, seen on 25 July 1962, from her unique deflectors, applied as a sequel to numerous smoke lifting experiments pre-war. She was withdrawn in August 1963.

Plate 84: A trip on the ferry provided an opportunity to study the massive cantilever columns, twelve feet in diameter, which spring from the base of the structure, and which permitted a 150 foot navigable headway. Even the subsidiary girders in this part of the structure seem dwarfed by these mighty erections, yet they too are larger than many main bridge girders elsewhere. Studying this view, we can see why the painting of the bridge was a continuous task. For those who like their feet firmly on the ground, it is also a daunting one!

Chapter 8

Southern Memories — The Isle of Wight

Plate 85: Sun, steam and holiday-makers were the ingredients one associated with the Isle of Wight. All three are here, as No. W32 *Bonchurch*, an Adams 02 class 0-4-4 tank, nears Ryde St John's Road with a Ventnor train on 20 August 1963, when the railway was still an important artery for the holiday makers. The overbridge, which adjoined the platform ends at Ryde St John's, restricted vantage points for photography, yet offered dramatic possibilities of steam, sun and shadow which were all too rarely exploited in colour. When this view was taken, steam services ran south from Ryde Pier Head to Shanklin and Ventnor, and west to Newport and Cowes, serving most of the important resorts and communities on the Island.

Plate 86: The railways of the Isle of Wight, though a part of BR, were separated from the mainland system by a narrow strip of water, which ensured that they were largely self contained as regarded workshops, rolling stock and operation. This isolation, coupled with loading gauge restrictions which precluded most modern stock, preserved a *pre-group* flavour. Although the livery was BR from 1948, a fleet of lovingly maintained Victorian tank engines hauled elderly timber bodied stock with never an 'outside' vehicle in sight. The survival into the era of colour photography of this delightful system – emphatically not a *backwater* – enabled one to savour a minor pre-grouping railway in many respects. Alas, only a minority of the enthusiasts to visit the Island, did so with colour film in their cameras. To small boys, a locomotive shed, ANY shed, was a mecca. Add veteran steam engines from Victorian times, and a school visit, and what better way to be educated? In August 1962, when school parties were still disciplined, and actually looked smart, these youngsters learn about railways. No. 24 *Calbourne* and No. 31 *Chale* neatly frame this study of Ryde shed.

▼*Plate 87:* The running shed at Ryde St John's was built by the Southern Railway in 1930, and replaced the former Isle of Wight edifice. Compared to many steam sheds, it was well lit and spacious, and even after the closure of Newport shed in the 1950s, which increased its allocation by 50%, and severely over crowded the accommodation, the shed staff took a fierce pride in their charges, as evidenced by the condition of No. 20 *Shanklin* on 20 May 1964. By this time, a clean locomotive on the mainland was a novelty. On the Island, it was accepted as customary for engines to go into traffic like this. The third engine on this row, No. 29 *Alverstone*, is even better groomed. Pools of water in the foreground shew that the standpipes between the two shed roads have been in use recently. Today, just the Ryde – Shanklin section remains in use, worked by the former London Transport underground stock, and the days when the graceful Adams tanks hauled crowds of happy holiday makers are a memory. Happily a short section of the Newport line has been preserved, but rows of 02 tanks being prepared for duty is a sight we shall never again witness.

20

14

▲ *Plate 88:* No. W14 *Fishbourne*, built in December 1889, and the oldest 02 on the Island, blows off impatiently at the head of the 5.08pm ex Newport to Ryde on 21 August 1963, awaiting the arrival of a northbound train to clear the single line section. No. 14 was one of several engines fitted with metal shields round the Westinghouse air brake pump, to prevent oil splashing the windows of brake coaches when running bunker first. The guards liked it, but the pumps splashed themselves with oil, and the fitters did not; the fitters won!

Plate 89: The best known and most loved of all Isle of Wight engines, No. W24 *Calbourne* basks in the sun at Ryde St John's on 20 May 1964. Even then, *Calbourne* was a celebrity, boasting highly polished splasher beading, spectacle glass surrounds and nameplates, yet she was no coddled showpiece, as the slight patina of dirt, which tokens a hard worked engine earning her keep, demonstrates. Alone of the 02s, she has survived into preservation. What lovely engines they were.

Chapter 9

Southern Memories — The Bournemouth Line

Plate 90: A nocturnal study of Waterloo, terminus of the LSWR routes into London, and scene of many poignant departures. The signal box was part of the Southern modernisation, and opened in 1936 with 309 levers. One of the authors was an early visitor to this historic power box, but our portrait comes from thirty years later.

Plate 91: A signalman's view – A BR Standard class 3 2-6-2 tank, No. 82023, shunts milk tanks at Waterloo in the late autumnal sun on 1 November 1965. Although physical constraints sometimes ruled otherwise, a good view of the station 'throat' was desirable in mechanical and early power box working, and Waterloo box was admirably placed. The class 3 standard tank was intended for light branch duties and pilot work, and was largely designed at Swindon. The Western Region was the largest user, according them a form of honorary GWR status, on account of their parentage, but the North Eastern and Southern regions had a few, the latter often finding work around Waterloo, a legacy of the shortage of modern tanks on the Southern. As an aside to history, it was for duties such as this that Bulleid envisaged the *Leader*. With a different election result in 1945, this view might have been of a malachite green CC1, or one of her sisters. Thus is history altered.

35014

Plate 92 (Facing Page): The most powerful and dramatic of the Southern steam classes were the thirty *Merchant Navy* pacifics, the first of which were introduced when the merchant service was filling a vital war role. The original engines, with their air smoothed casings and chain driven valve gear, were all rebuilt by BR in the fifties, the most obvious visual alteration being the removal of the casing. The styling adopted for the rebuilds resulted in their becoming a more graceful version of the BR Standard pacifics. No. 35014 *Nederland Line* blows off vigorously, as she heads a Bournemouth express beneath one of the London & South Western pneumatic signal gantries at the west end of Basingstoke station on 29 October 1965. In their rebuilt form, the locomotives were a fascinating mixture of Bulleid's ideas and BR thinking, not least the curious oval smokebox door, which was a legacy from the original design. This three quarters angle reveals a design feature common to many locomotive classes in latter years. When the railways were being established, locomotives and carriages were diminutive, and the loading gauge correspondingly small. By the time it was realised that a more generous loading gauge would have been an asset, it was too late. Other countries profited by the mistake, with better structure gauges from the start. Overall height and width limitations are well understood. What many enthusiasts overlook is that throw-over clearances on curves could often be critical, and front and rear overhangs played a major part in design. This is apparent on the rebuilt Bulleid pacifics in the reduction in width of the running plate ahead of the cylinders.

Plate 93 (Above): Appropriately for a class which enjoyed such a flamboyant career, the *Merchant Navies* carried some of the most striking locomotive nameplates ever created. Spare a moment though, for the grease and oil on the running plate.

In 1937, had anyone given prolonged thought to the demise of British steam, and in more detail, which company and which route would claim the distinction of Britain's last steam-worked main line, it is highly improbable that the Southern Railway would have been a serious candidate. The company had retained many elderly steam locomotives, but this was not because of a devotion to steam, but the exact opposite; electric traction was the apple in the Southern eye, and one could anticipate a steady spread of electric route mileage westwards, once the principal Eastern and Central section routes had been dealt with, a process well advanced by the late thirties. In that year, the Southern had gained a new CME, Oliver Vaughan Snell Bulleid. He had come from the LNER, and was an unknown quantity.

A decade later, Bulleid was no longer an unknown quantity; he had created two of the most spectacular pacific classes ever to run in Britain, a remarkable class of 0-6-0 freight engines, and was working on a bogie steam locomotive of revolutionary concept. Even so, the Southern would hardly have been the front runner, for Southern management had announced plans to slash its 1,800 steam locomotives to 800, with a vast expansion of electrified mileage, and many other routes worked by diesel power. The Bulleid steam, already past the 100 mark, would provide the backbone of Southern steam, but would be a final fling, its sphere of operation gradually retiring westwards as diesel and electric mileage increased.

Nationalisation changed all that; the Railway Executive was steam orientated, and the Southern vision of an array of diesel or electric locomotives withered. The construction of Bulleid classes soon came to an end, but standards were appearing in growing numbers. At that point, as we have seen, the RE ceased to exist, and modernisation became the goal, at first orderly and cautious, then a mad scramble. Routes were to be dieselised or electrified. The Midland main line, which was to be diesel in the long term, was an early casualty. The West Coast Main Line, to be electrified, acquired a leavening of diesels, but steam lived on until electrification. On the Southern, the Waterloo – Bournemouth route was also to be electrified, but with the need for diesels elsewhere, and the fleet of modern pacifics built by Bulleid in less than a decade, the switch would be direct, from steam to electric. The electrification took considerable time, and thus it was, in the mid-sixties, that the Waterloo Bournemouth line became the last predominantly steam worked main line in the British Isles. Steam workings came to an end in July 1967; it is true that other pockets of steam were to exist for another year, but these were in areas where the diesel predominated, and steam turns were often a minority. Between them, the Southern management, Oliver Bulleid, Adolf Hitler, the Labour Party, and the Modernisation Plan had made the absurdity of 1937 into the reality of 1967. Had Southern logic held sway, the pacifics which pounded through the New Forest in the mid-sixties, would have been confined to the West Country long since.

Plate 94: In Plates 24-26, we looked at mechanical signalling, as practised by the London & North Western Railway, and with modifications, by virtually every other railway in the land. Today, we live in the era of the power box, working scores or hundreds of track miles. Power signalling is not a new idea however. In the early 1900s, the London & South Western was a progressive and ambitious company, and following a visit to the United states by the engineer, J W Jacomb-Hood, and the superintendent of the Line, Sam Fay (later to become Sir Sam Fay of GCR fame), the LSWR opted for low pressure pneumatic operation of signals and points, the important quadruple track section from Woking to Basingstoke being an early installation. This carried the Bournemouth as well as the West of England traffic, and the system soon proved its value. The number and size of boxes were reduced, staffing economies made, and smoother operation permitted. This early power installation survived until electrification. In plate 94, we see Basingstoke station looking towards Waterloo on 29 October 1965. The GW line to Reading diverges to the left; in the 'V' of the junction is the BR power box which replaced the LSWR installation in 1966, including Basingstoke A box, visible on the extreme right. The pneumatic cylinders powering the signals are attached to the post below each arm, whilst pipework replaces the usual rodding and counterweights.

Plate 96: The frames were provided by the British Pneumatic Railway Signal Co., and the 'levers' were steel slides about 17 inches in length, with a detachable handle at one end which the signalman pulled or pushed. Within the frame, the slide was cut to a complex pattern, activating tappet locking and the pneumatic system itself. Handles were coloured in the normal way, and spares were produced by means of a white handle, or latterly by just removing it entirely. When the authors inspected the Basingstoke installation in its last months, they were first presented with a handle, and then with a complete 'lever', which had been extracted from the frame during alterations. Few signalling systems possessed the attraction of 'give-away' levers.

Plate 95: With mechanical signalling, the distance at which points could be worked from a box was limited by Board of Trade rules in many cases, whilst the physical effort needed to pull a point and its associated rodding, was another limitation. Large stations were worked by numerous boxes at close intervals, and this added further problems, with dual or multiple operation of one signal by several boxes, known as slotting. A slotted signal could become very heavy to pull whilst the signal fitter's job was a nightmare. Power working enabled points and signals to be worked at much greater distances, so reducing the number of boxes needed, cutting down on manpower, and on slotting. The power frames only occupied half the length of a mechanical installation, permitting a much smaller cabin, as is apparent with the 60 'lever' Basingstoke A frame.

31639

▲*Plate 97:* Although the Bulleid pacifics dominated Bournemouth workings latterly, aided by an influx of BR standards, an earlier era lingered into 1966, with the last of the Maunsell mixed traffic moguls. No. 31639, one of the last U class moguls to be built, in 1931, makes a spirited departure from Brockenhurst with a Bournemouth train on 10 June 1965, a year prior to her demise.

Plate 98: The Bulleid pacifics possessed a high power:weight ratio. Whilst this maximised route availability, it made them prone to slip on starting, and one of the experiences of steam was to see and hear a Merchant Navy struggling to get away with a heavy train, her wheels spinning, and her exhaust merging into a roaring cacophony. No. 35030 *Elder Dempster Lines* has her steam sanders on, as she struggles to keep her feet, getting a westbound train away from Brockenhurst.

Plate 99: Overleaf, we discussed one of the 'moments' of the steam age. Watching any powerful express locomotive, but particularly a pacific, getting a heavy express train under way was a fascinating experience. The driver would ease open the regulator, and imperceptibly, the train would begin to move — always present was the lurking threat of too hasty an acceleration, or a greasy rail leading to a thunderous bout of slipping. At night, with the ruddy glare from the fire bathing the cab in angry tones of red and orange, steam could achieve demoniacal mien. A chilly day in winter, with a fresh fall of snow was another such experience. In plate 31, we illustrated steam and snow in sunshine, with a crisp well compacted snow. Here we look back to the late afternoon of a Spring day in the New Forest in 1966. It is April, but to the intense disgust of local residents, a coating of snow has whitened the countryside. The signalman at Hinton Admiral, snug in his LSWR signal box part way along the platform, has pulled off. A cold vigil is rewarded a few minutes later, as No. 34057 *Biggin Hill* an unrebuilt Battle of Britain pacific, powers through the station, her exhaust condensing in the chill air, whilst the powdery snow billows up in her wake. Moments later the signals will have gone back to danger, and except for a momentary smell of steam and hot oil, the authors will be left to their lonely task until the next train comes. What will it be? A Merchant Navy; or a 'spam can' to quote the undignified name bestowed by many upon Bulleid's pacifics; perhaps it will be a standard. In summer or in winter, fair weather or foul, that was the question uppermost in one's mind. The last train had gone; what would come next. In today's world of preserved steam, locomotives are far cleaner and better groomed than was the case for many years. Modern SLR cameras and high speed films permit photography which would have been a dream in the heyday of steam. No one would deny that preserved steam photography is exciting, yet at the same time, one misses the sense that what we have just seen was an ordinary everyday occasion, with a locomotive doing its intended job. We also miss the anticipation of what WOULD come next. Often it was a disappointment in the latter months of steam, but that made the excitement all the more intense the next time round. Indeed, it was all rather like a game of cricket, exciting to watch in the re-play, but definitely more so, when the stroke was yet to be played. The sense that one was living through a moment never to be repeated was ever present, as if one was watching the declared last innings of a great batsman inching towards a long desired goal.

▼*Plate 100:* As No. 34079, *141 Squadron*, an unrebuilt Battle of Britain pacific waits time at Bournemouth Central with a Weymouth to Waterloo Express on 11 June 1966, we can take a leisurely look at the lines of these remarkable engines, for as her sister *Biggin Hill* roared past us in a haze of steam and snow, we barely had time to make out her number, let alone study her in detail. Here was another pardox of the steam age. The steam locomotive was at its most dramatic, tearing along at the head of an express train, or slogging away in front of an endless vista of four wheel wagons, yet to gain more than a fleeting impression, it was to the stopping places or sheds that one turned. In this portrait of steam, we have sought to blend the action with the detailed portrait, to suit the lover of the dramatic, and those who would linger. To the modeller, a close look at the varied hues of the steam engine is always a fascination. Look at the motion with its rich covering of oil and grease, coal dust and road dirt. Let your eye wander to the staining on the casing by the firebox or to the smearing of grime upon the cab or tender flanks. This is what Britain's last steam main line was like, fascinating, doomed, but an era to live through. The original 141 squadron flew Bolton Paul Defiant twin seat fighters during the battle, one of only two squadrons so equipped.

BOURNEMOUTH CENTRAL
141 SQUADRON
34079
34079

Chapter 10

Branch Line Miscellany

Far removed from the hectic pace of the main lines was the world of the country branch line. Trains were neither plentiful nor very large; locomotives and stock were neither large nor modern, and they assuredly did not hurtle by at the pace of the main line expresses. A slow steady plod would be a better description. Just as the main line had its devotees, who would turn up their noses at the rural backwaters, so did the branch lines have their followers, or, as with the authors, one could savour both worlds. The 'branch' took its name from analogy with the tree, coming off the main stem, and many pleasant lines terminated in peaceful little towns or villages. Others meandered across country from one junction to another.

Their character was made up not just of the trains which pottered along from station to station, their crews, the station staffs and regular passengers all knowing one another, or even the pretty little buildings with their trim flowerbeds. These were the visible manifestations of the branch line, and the things which *could* be recorded on film. There was much which could never be captured in this way. The location hardly matters, but journey back in time to coal fires in the grate, and a cold winter's day, with a cherry red fire glowing in the booking office hearth, and the meagre glow from an ailing scattering of embers in the waiting room fire. As an aside to modellers, should you ever add smoke effects to your buildings, DO remember this point — the reverse would be as likely as a pink 'Castle'. The branch line signalbox, especially if it happened to be on the platform, served as a social centre for the railwaymen, and as often as not, the neighbours as well. One memory of long ago was of elevenses at a little branch box in the West Country, a process which included the signalman, booking clerk, various railwaymen who just 'happened' to be around at the time. Various neighbours popped in, and a seal of approval was accorded by the presence of the station master, whose lady presided! It was not strictly in accordance with the rule book, but officialdom was a long way off. Then again, there was the booking clerk at a minor North Western station who had reasoned that as Monday mornings were busy, and nobody ever travelled on a Saturday afternoon, that Saturday lunchtime was a good moment to change the date stamp. On the main lines, the signalman might seldom have time to visit his 'little house' — on the branch lines, it was rather different. There is one story, probably true, on the narrow gauge, of a hurriedly arranged inspection train being held up because the station master and staff had gone swimming, whilst one of the authors encountered a signalman he knew walking along the lineside carrying the successful results of a rabbit snaring expedition. As there were no trains . . .!

Life was often free and easy on the branch lines, and working hours by no means given over wholly to work. By the same token, the village station master was a leading figure in the community, and if an excursion was planned, had 'ways' of promoting it in the village. Many station masters kept a semi-private oddments book, which they might bequeath to a successor, if on good terms. In the early 1900s, the LNWR station master at Napton & Stockton kept such a book. He noted that posters should go to a local factory, two schools and three Women's Institutes. Excursion bills went to three local vicars, four school masters, a couple of local clubs and to a few people 'by placing under strings of parcels for delivery'. A note, improbably entered under K, mentioned that details of the local co-op were entered under W. In a large station that would have been confusing; at Napton, everyone knew to look up Co-op under W. The signalmen at one country box, sometimes worked by reliefmen, who were suspected of being heavy handed with the communal tea supply, had an even more ingenious *filing* system, using a part of the block equipment, which was only supposed to be opened by the linesman, as a tea store!

The placid and unhurried nature of life on the branches gave them their special charm, yet it gave railway managers recurrent headaches, and sealed the fate of these delightful byeways. The lot of so many local railways, frequently financed by local people, was financial ruin and sale to one of their larger neighbours at a fraction of their cost. At the grouping one could gain some idea of how parlous many lines were, with costs rising even at that time. For every £100 ordinary stock in the Wick & Lybster Light Railway, shareholders received £12 10s in cash. For a like holding of Knott End ordinary stock, one received £6 5s of LMS ordinary stock. With road traffic cutting into revenue and costs rising, the branch line was under threat even between the wars, and in 1948, £100 of Shropshire & Montgomeryshire Railway ordinary stock was valued at five *shillings* (25p), putting the *entire railway* within the pocket of most enthusiasts! The reckoning came in the fifties and sixties.

One can record the branch engine or station, but no-one has yet invented a machine to capture the human atmosphere, or the brave but often unfulfilled hopes which were behind so many lines. In studying these portraits, ponder on what lies hidden.

1145 Gt Western Ry H.M. FORCES ON LEAVE TORQUAY to PADDINGTON 1 Via Taunton FIRST CLASS | Gt Western Ry H.M. FORCES ON LEAVE Paddington 1 to TORQUAY Via Taunton FIRST CLASS | FOR CONDITIONS SEE BACK W.D 1145

0957 L.N.E.R. EXCESS FARE COLLECTED. HORNSEA to HULL Difference between 3rd & 1st Class Ordinary Single Available on day of issue only See back Fare X.S.S. 3258 10d.N FIRST HULL CLASS 0957

▼*Plate 101:* The Kingswear branch of the GWR was celebrated amongst railfans long before preservation as the Torbay & Dartmouth Railway. The fireman is busy turning his black liveried prairie tank, still with the early Lion emblem, in this long vanished scene. Visitors of today will mourn the passing of the turntable, loco and carriage roads and other facilities.

72
41295

▲*Plate 102:* Rather than dart from branch to branch, with a myriad of confusing impressions, we have decided to 'star' one such line, the LSWR Lymington branch, which earned brief renown as the last 'classic' steam branch on BR. Most branches served a local community, or perhaps a holiday resort, in which the terminus was the destination of its passengers. A few, including the Lymington branch, were a link in the transport chain, connecting, in this case, with the ferry to the Isle of Wight. Except for the odd through working, branch trains commenced or terminated at Brockenhurst, a pleasant town on the edge of the New Forest. No. 41295, an Ivatt *Mickey Mouse* 2-6-2 tank, leaves Brockenhurst with a two coach train of Southern region green stock on 11 June 1965. A wagon is undergoing repairs in the yard.

Plate 103: The Lymington branch diverged from the main Waterloo Bournemouth line at Lymington Junction, a delightful location about a mile south west of Brockenhurst. The picturesque LSWR cabin once controlled the junction with the Ringwood line as well, but the only trace of this is a third post, minus signal arm, on the splitting signal beyond the overbridge. The main line arm is higher than the branch signal to indicate relative importance. There is also a speed limit sign on to the branch. The two white posts in the foreground are the single line staff exchange apparatus. A platform is provided for the signalman to hand the staff over to trains entering the single track section, whilst there is a third post by the box for mechanical hand over.

Plate 104: Lymington Town, the only intermediate station, was on the west bank of the Lymington river, and served the local community. The branch tank was housed in a diminutive shed just beyond the platform. Similar sheds were once numerous, each with their own primitive coaling stage. The use of old sleepers in both the stage and the adjoining hut was a customary economy in the use of material, and whilst second hand sleepers and corrugated iron were hardly stylish, they lasted, and they were cheap!

Plate 105: The line terminated at Lymington Pier, partly on land, and partly over water, passengers walking a few yards to board the ferries for the 4 mile trip to Yarmouth IOW. Departing trains hugged the east bank of the Lymington river for a short distance, before crossing to the far bank via a low bridge. No. 41312, a *Mickey Mouse* now preserved in South Wales, makes a vigorous departure from the Pier station on 30 October 1966, her exhaust condensing in the crisp autumnal air, as the signalman reluctantly leaves the warmth of his box to hand over the single line staff. At high tide, the sea laps within a couple of feet of the tufts of wiry grass in the foreground. Poignancy is given to this traditional scene by the brand new white insulator 'pots' for the electric third rail which was to banish steam within a few months.

Plate 106: One of the last steam worked branches in Ireland was the now lifted Great Northern line from Goraghwood on the Dublin – Belfast main line, via Newry, to the popular seaside resort of Warrenpoint. UTA No. 66, once GNR(I) No. 201 *Meath*, a class U 4-4-0, built as late as 1948, pauses at Newry (Edward St) Station in September 1964, when heading a rake of excursion stock towards Warrenpoint tender first. Although No. 201 was short enough to be turned at Warrenpoint, some classes required short tenders or much fiddling, one of many restrictions found on branches throughout the British Isles. Lamps were still allocated to individual engines.

Chapter 11

The End Draws Nigh

Our story opened with steam in firm control in the 1930s, with green liveried Southern 4-6-0s, or 'Red Staniers' on the LMS. We have seen the grime of World War II, and the dawn of BR, with a host of new liveries, such as Express Blue or carmine and cream. We have looked back to the confident announcement of a range of new standard types with service lives of 30 to 50 years. Had the plot followed those lines, we would not have needed to write this chapter, or at least for many years. Alas the plot thickened in the early fifties; the RE was swept away, and with it, the total commitment to steam. Dieselisation and electrification were the motive power of the future, and after careful trial, would 'largely supersede' steam. The careful trial soon went by the board, and an inter-regional race to dieselise began. The last BR steam locomotive, No. 92220 *Evening Star* rolled out of Swindon works in 1960. Once there had been no urgency, for there was always tomorrow or next year or the year after. Then selected classes became favourites, but a mere Hall or Black Five might pass by with hardly a camera being raised.

As the end drew nearer in each region, and indeed for each group of lines, the chase became ever more desperate. Days by the lineside, or 'on shed' were looked forward to with anticipation, and with a fervent hope, usually only experienced by the followers of the winning side in a test match, that 'tomorrow' would be fine. Unlike cricket, neither rain nor bad light stopped play, but it did make life miserable and the photographs, especially colour, less exciting. The majority of enthusiasts relied not just upon the 'mags', but on the 'grapevine' as well. Sometimes misleading, the grapevine often provided useful tips only days or hours old, and by the mid sixties, days often mattered. Workings which had been steam one week, turned out to be diesel on a return visit, and one more bastion had fallen. *Westerns*, *Warships*, *Peaks* or *Deltics* did not attract the indifference once reserved for mundane steam classes; the great majority of enthusiasts quite simply detested them. The 'faithful' compared notes with friends of many years, or acquaintances met for the first time whilst sharing the same pile of ash on shed taking indentical views of a run down standard, which would hardly have merited a glance a short while previously. Identical normally meant that both were 'loaded' with BW, for colour remained a minority appeal still. Human nature being what it is, a spirit of friendly rivalry grew up as to who could photograph the most survivors of a particular class before it was too late, but unlike many so-called sporting fixtures of to-day, where sportsmanship is the last consideration in the determination to win, helpful tips were given to 'rivals' and received thankfully. The columns of the various magazines waxed hot as the defenders of different areas claimed theirs as the 'best' in steam terms, and whilst dozens of steam movements had been the rule in an hour at the start of the sixties, by the mid-sixties, half a dozen steam workings in an hour were regarded as exciting. Those who photographed steam during this period will have their own favourite lineside. By early 1967, the 'best' areas had contracted to the north west or north east or the Waterloo Bournemouth line. That summer Waterloo – Bournemouth fell to electrification, and the choice narrowed further.

The official view was that all was going well, though there were those in BR who had qualms at the race into modernisation, and the piecemeal way in which it was effected. The official mind soothed these worries 'the first effect of modernisation works is often to lower the standard of service temporarily and to inflate operating costs . . . In particular, the maximum economies from the use of diesel and electric locomotives will not be achieved until they have completly replaced steam traction in the areas concerned'. The decline and fall of steam is graphically portrayed in tabular form.

BRITISH RAILWAYS MOTIVE POWER

Date	Steam	Diesel	Electric
31-12-60	13,276	2,550	135
31-12-61	11,691	3,179	158
31-12-62	8,767	3,683	178
31-12-63	7,050	4,060	194
31-12-64	4,973	4,462	198
31-12-65	2,987	4,811	277
31-12-66	1,689	4,962	340
31-12-67	362	4,742	341
31-12-68	3	4,326	329

These figures, although dramatic in themselves, do not tell the whole story, for the vast fleet of DMUs, operating in two three or four car formations, or even longer trains, added a fresh dimension to dieselisation, with 3,820 DMU vehicles in 1960, and after an increase in the middle years, 3810 at the close of 1968.

Save for the seasonally-worked tourist-orientated Vale of Rheidol narrow gauge section, it was all over by the end of 1968. What were those last days on BR like, and elsewhere in the British Isles. Having painted in the backdrop, we will watch the players as the last curtain falls.

Plate 107: Athough the diesel locomotive offered the principal threat to steam, and massively outnumbered electric locomotives in the sixties, electrification schemes, with the steady advance of overhead or third rail power supply long before the change-over, seemed to posess an even more stark threat to steam. The diesel might come, but frequently it was in small numbers gradually eroding steam turns. With electrification, the switch was sudden and usually total. A Stanier 8F, No. 48493 heads a one/fifth fitted class 6 freight of about sixty wagons southbound along the quadruple track Trent Valley Main Line near Newbold on 20 July 1963. The early, and rather cumbersome overhead structures have been erected; the catenary has yet to be hung, but the menace is there.

'In the Office' — The steam locomotive did not exist in isolation, for a complex maintenance and administrative machine was required to keep it in traffic, to ensure that it received regular and special attention, fuel, oil and water, and a crew for its assigned duty. A vast range of forms had to be kept at every shed, ranging from staff holidays, through the level of spare parts, to locomotive records. The 'X' Examination and Repair Card for a Stanier 8F No. 48757 for a single examination is a reminder of the activity which went on behind the scenes to keep the wheels rolling during the Steam Age. Old traditions die hard, and the staff at Crewe South have referred to the Stanier by her 'LMS' number, 8757, simply by dropping the BR '4', overlooking the fact that this engine was built for the LNER as a war-time emergency measure.

BRITISH TRANSPORT COMMISSION
BRITISH RAILWAYS

B.R. 32990/2

"X" EXAMINATION & REPAIR CARD

DATE 10/9/64 Date of last "X" Repair 21-8-64 ENGINE No. 8757
Crewe South Depot TENDER No. ......

Item No.	PARTS TO BE EXAMINED	Standard Time Hr. Min.	Team T. M.	Date	Check No.	Time On Hr. Min.	Time Off Hr. Min.	S.Ms. Per Actual Team	Examiners Initials
	Examine in Steam-All repairs to be booked on reverse side								
1 X	Steam cocks & joints in cab & steam manifold								
2 X	Brake system	84	1	10/9/64	1914			3/4	JB
3 X	All joints in smokebox								
4 X	Cylinder cocks & gear								
5 X	Steam sanding apparatus								
6 X	Condenser gear								
7 X	Injectors & pipe joints								
8 X	Compressed air controlled regulator gear								
9 X	Coal pusher								
11 X	All flexible pipes, other than lubrication system								
12 X	Graduable steam brake valve								
	Examine-out of Steam-All repairs to be booked on reverse side								
13 X	General examination by Examining Fitter with special reference to the following items:-	50	1	10/9/64	1914			8 0	JB
14 X	Axlebox wedges								
15 X	Oil pipes and oil pipe clips								
16 X	Spring and spring gear								
17 X	Nose snow ploughs								

Item No.	The following items to be examined and receive attention as laid down in the "Schedule of 'X' Examinations"	Standard Time Hr. Min.	Team T. M.	Date	Tradesman Check No.	Time On Hr. Min.	Time Off Hr. Min.	Mate and/or Apprentice Check No.	Time On Hr. Min.	Time Off Hr. Min.	S.Ms./ Actual Team	Repair Code No.
18 X	Tender Tank, side and saddle tank	12	T	10/9/64	1913			X				
19 X	Combined external water feed valve and sieve	12	T	10/9/64	1913			X				
20 X	Tender or tank water pick-up apparatus	26	T	10/9/64	1913			X				
21 X	Blast pipe, blower ring, exhaust pipe from ejector or Westinghouse pump	1 04	T	10/9/64	1913			X				
22 X	Compressed air controlled regulator gear											
23 X	Coal pusher											
24 X	Axlebox underkeeps with drain plugs, filling holes and removable covers	2 23	T	11/9/64	1913			1961			11 3/2	
25 X	Axlebox trimmings and oil boxes. Piston and valve spindle swabs	36	T	10/9/64	1913			X				
26 X	Grease nipples, except on roller bearing axleboxes	1 41	T	10/9/64	1913							
27 X	Vacuum controlled regulator gear (Push/Pull locomotives)											
28 X	Mechanically controlled regulator gear (Push/Pull locomotives)											
29 X	Timken roller bearing (Oil lubricated)											
30 X	Motion oil bath											
31 X	Caprotti Lentz and other poppet valve gears											
32 X	Smokebox internal deflector plates											
33 X	Rocker grate and drop grate											
34 X	Hopper ashpan and damper gear fittings	22	T	10/9/64	1913			X			27 3	
35 X	Gravity sanding apparatus											
36 X	A.W.S. apparatus (L.T.S. System)											
38 X	Speed indicator											
39 X	Graduable Steam brake valve											
40 X	Brake gear	10	T	10/9/64	1913			X				
41 X	Overhead electrification warning flashes	08	T	10/9/64	1913			X				

Entered

B.R. 32990/2—Back.

REPAIRS REQUIRED (One item only to be entered on each line) Deferred/Booked/Arising from Exam	Standard Time Hr. Min.	Team T. M.	Date	Tradesman Check No.	Time On Hr. Min.	Time Off Hr. Min.	Mate and/or Apprentice Check No.	Time On Hr. Min.	Time Off Hr. Min.	S.Ms./ Actual Team	Repair Code No.
Regulator gland packing	1 14	T	10/9/64	1913			X				
Both injector gland packing	38	T	10/9/64	1913			X				
Large & small ejector nuts packing	16	T	10/9/64	1913			X			16 5	
Brake steam valve nut packing	08	T	10/9/64	1913			X				
Jet valve spindle nut packing	09	T	10/9/64	1913			X				
Steam sander blows through	20	T	10/9/64	1913			X				
Both side gauge cock nuts blowing	2 12	T	10/9/64	1913			1961				
Atomiser steam pipe nut blows	16	T	10/9/64	1913			1961				
Atomiser steam valve spindle nut packing	1 00	T	10/9/64	1913			1961			43 8	
Right side piston packing blows	4 00	T	10/9/64	1913			1961				
Engine brake adjusting	14	T	11/9/64	1913			1961				
Tender " "	35	T	11/9/64	1913			1961				
Tank feed glands leaking	2 06	T	11/9/64	1913			1961				
Right side coupling rod joint pin nut loose	28	T	11/9/64	1913			1961				
Right side tank feed handle very loose on quadrant	45	T	11/9/64	1928			1951			45 2	
Examination of engine and tender and steam test after "X" repairs	30	1	11/9/64	1915						3 0	

Entered

MATERIAL USED

DATE	DESCRIPTION OR CATALOGUE No.	QUANTITY
10/9/64	1 piston packing spring	
10/9/64	Regulator Gland packing	
11/9/64	Axle oil	

SIGNATURE OF MECHANICAL FOREMAN OR LEADING FITTER H Lynch DATE 11-9-64

94
49078

▲ *Plate 108:* Waiting the torch: – No. 49078, an LNWR eight coupled goods is rusted and grimy, and her battered running plate is evidence of less than gentle encounters with other engines and with freight stock during her long service career. A few of these engines were active into 1964, but not No. 49078 which we see on 13 July, at Rugby shed. Her presence there, many months after withdrawal, recalls an amusing incident of the switch from steam to electric power on the West Coast Main Line. As the time drew near to energise the wires south of Crewe, instructions were issued to shed masters to produce full lists of motive power on hand, so that arrangements could be made to withdraw or transfer classes, which could not safely operate under the 25kV overhead, away from the electrified sections. The Stanier Duchess pacifics were one such prohibited class; Jubilees and Scots were similarly listed. When the Rugby shed master was preparing his list, he included details of No. 49078, the last surviving ex LNWR locomotive in the area. According to the powers-that-be, No. 49078 did not *exist* any longer, and the shed master was firmly reprimanded for his error. His insistence that he truly did have an LNWR 0-8-0, and that they could come and look at it if they didn't believe him, caused much upset, and arrangements were speedily made to remove the offending machine forthwith. As No. 49078, which still carries the old lion and wheel emblem, had been in store at Rugby for a very long time indeed, authority may perhaps be excused their error, but what a shame they *ever* discovered it. These eight coupled freights, the first being built by F W Webb in small boilered guise, provided the mainstay of LNWR heavy freight services from the late 1890s to the grouping, and until the multiplication of the Stanier 2-8-0s, of the Western Division of the LMS. Even in the 1960s, No. 49078 had not received the brackets, let alone the smokebox door number plate which was LMS and BR policy!

Plate 109: A flashback in time to happier days, as a sister engine, LMS No. 9146, shunts a timber bodied coal wagon near the British Thompson Houston works, Rugby, about 1947. At this time LMS steam was badly run down, and only the numerals and tender lettering have been cleaned. It will be seen that No. 9146 has been equipped with a tender cab, a useful addition for an engine which might have to do a certain amount of shunting or tender first running. In the background are some of the old tall sided coke wagons which were once so much a part of the railway scene. Clearly the LMS had been no more successful with No. 9146 and smokebox door plates than BR was destined to be with No. 49078. From Webb's original design of 1892, the LNWR 8-coupled goods was developed by Whale, Bowen-Cooke and Beames in turn. Their introduction boosted LNWR freight trains from 30-40 wagons to 60 or more, and saved much double heading or expensive additional running lines. They epitomised the Crewe tradition of cheap mass produced engines, simple to build and operate, but with a good service life. Many lasted 50 or 60 years.

HELLIFIELD

Plate 110: As the size and variety of the BR steam fleet dwindled under the triple onslaught of diesel, electric, and the Beeching closures, enthusiasm grew, and by 1965 the prospect of a steam special with an *interesting* class guaranteed a good turnout of participants and photographers en route. A new term eventually came into being for the latter, 'linesiders', and at photostops, the mass of participants and linesiders often made it extremely difficult to photograph the object at the centre of this new form of hero worship. Until early 1964, LMSR 'Royal Scots' had been plentiful, but the dieselisation of the Midland main line, and electrification of the WCML, saw their ranks decimated. Only five Scots survived into 1965, ensuring the kind of welcome No. 46115 *Scots Guardsman* would receive when she entered Hellifield station from the Blackburn line with an RCTS Special in February 1965. The diagonal yellow stripe on the cabside was a warning symbol to indicate that No. 46115, in common with a number of other LMR classes, was not to work under the 25kV live wires south of Crewe after 1 September 1964. The short February days, low winter sun, and often dull conditions of the Settle Carlisle route in winter, made an unlikely timing for such an event, but with scores of engines 'going' every month, even February days could not be cast aside. As it happened, No. 46115 had almost a year to live in BR service, for she was not withdrawn until January 1966, and then, it was for preservation. At the time, however, the preservation movement had not grown to the extent it has subsequently reached, and the limited number of 'schemes' that did exist seemed to be in danger of overtaxing the enthusiast pocket of the day. As a result, many classes were lost, and perhaps a single example survived of others. Had they survived just a little longer, would two of the Adams Radial tanks have gone to the Scrap man, or every Patriot, County or Peppercorn A1? No. 46115 survives, but she was one of the lucky ones, and so many classes did not.

Plate 111: As the BR network contracted, and the scrap lines lengthened, silence fell upon engine sheds throughout the land. Not many years prior to this portrait being taken, Hellifield shed had echoed to the myriad sounds of a busy loco depot, and the smells of smoke, steam and hot oil had wafted across the tracks. Hellifield station, the junction of the MR Skipton to Lancaster/Carnforth lines and the LYR Blackburn branch pre-dated the Settle Carlisle line by many years, but gained its fame from the Long Drag. Generations of enginemen battled with the gradients and weather of this spectacular route, and the shed boasted a pair of massive wedge snow ploughs for decades. Closure came on 17 June 1963; in the ordinary course of events, demolition would have ensued, but with the growing collection of officially preserved locomotives, the shed was made reasonably weatherproof and vandalproof and served as a store to a mixture of motive power, some contemporary with its own completion in Victorian times, and others far more modern. Eventually this use came to an end, and the shed lay idle once again. To walk through the deserted shed, silent save for the cooing of the pigeons, or disconcerting echo of one's footsteps, was an eerie feeling. When the authors last visited the site, grass and rubble alone remained.

Plate 112: The Last Steam Main Line – No. 34036 *Westward Ho*, a Bulleid 'West Country' pacific, bursts out of the gloom of Holdenhurst Road bridge on the last few yards of the journey to Bournemouth Central on 11 June 1963. Once an Exmouth Junction engine, she had been transferred eastwards, following the WR take-over in those parts. The Bournemouth line provided a refuge for a few years, then . . .

▼*Plate 113:* As the evening shadows lengthen, and the setting sun paints the scene with colours worthy of a Turner impression, a tired BR 'Standard', No. 73119 *Elaine*, named after the Fair Maid of the Arthurian legend, pulls out of Bournemouth Central on 28 October 1966. Ill-kempt and neglected, steam approached the Twilight of the Gods, its fascination undimmed to those who knew it.

POST
OFFICE
250

1Z79
44874
CARNFOR

Plate 114: By the summer of 1968, BR steam workings had shrunk to a handful of turns provided by Rose Grove (Burnley), Lostock Hall and Carnforth Sheds. These ran for the last time on Saturday 3 August. The following morning, Lostock Hall shed turned out no fewer than nine locomomotives for the SIX farewell specials scheduled to run that day, as thousands of participants and linesiders were to take part in a unique 'experience'. The Stephenson Locomotive Society had arranged two double headed specials, one with Nos. 44871 and 44894, the other with Nos. 44874 and 45017, all four being Stanier 'Black Fives'. The latter special is seen at Blackburn. The commendable state of the locomotives is the result of a great deal of hard work put in by enthusiasts and a few railwaymen to ensure that steam went out with elegance, and not grimy and rust streaked, as had been increasingly the case from 1965. One of the L&Y water tanks has already lost its hose, and they, in common with the remaining infrastructure of the steam age would soon be no more.

Plate 115: A week later, on Sunday 11 August 1968, the bleak uplands of the Settle – Carlisle route witnessed a tumult of human activity unequalled since the halcyon days ninety years earlier, when the line was being built. Enthusiasts came by car, by van, and even by double decker bus, to the remote places to pay homage for the last time. No. 70013 *Oliver Cromwell*, the only Britannia pacific still active, sweeps through Ribblehead station at the head of the multi-coloured 'Fifteen Guinea Special', the bare northern fells making a strange contrast with the excitement nearer the station in this evocative panorama. Other engines used on different legs of the journey were Nos. 45110, 44871 and 44781. Immense numbers turned out at the famous vantage points, whilst at stops the engines were surrounded by a milling crowd. BR posters proclaimed 'This will be the very last train to operate on standard gauge track headed by a BR Steam Locomotive', with a headline, 'British Rail Runs out of steam'.

Plate 116: For years, the scrapyards had been working flat out to 're-cycle' a million tons of British steam power, for such was the BR fleet once! Not even the heat of a glorious July day, or familiarity with similar scenes elsewhere, could dispel the chill atmosphere of this scrap yard near Wigan, where a row of LMSR 2-6-4 tanks were to be found in 1964. Boiler tubes and the wreckage of once proud engines litter the foreground. In the distance, a heap of fireboxes offer mute testimony that others have been this way before. How many days or hours before these four locomotives join that tragic mound of metal? A row of tank wagon bodies show that other work has been tackled.

Plate 117: Not all scrapmen were so speedy in their work. In South Wales, row upon row of steam locomotives lay still, year after year, and as liveries and lettering faded, nature painted in vivid colours of her own, the stark red-brown of rust, and the lush green of fresh grass finding a foothold in the coaldust and slack of a previous era. No. 30825 is a 5ft. 7in. Maunsell S15 mixed traffic 4-6-0. Her location, as many readers will guess, is Woodham Brothers' scrapyard in Barry. The survival for so long of so many locomotives was due to other scrap contracts, and the Barry time-machine provided the nucleus of steam power to create a new steam age, the preservation era.

Plate 118: With the spotlight so firmly focused on BR in 1967-68, developments elsewhere tended to go un-noticed. Mostly, these were for the worse, but steam won a temporary reprieve in Ulster, and a major haulage contract! In the sixties the Ulster authorities embarked upon a motorway programme, amongst which was the M2, from Belfast to Larne. This would involve considerable land reclamation, and as both the tipping site and the quarry site adjoined the UTA, rail haulage was agreed upon. The first spoil train ran on 5 December 1966, and soon there were five workings each way, and by 1969, there were eleven return trips daily. It was not economical to build new motive power for a limited life, although a fleet of vacuum braked hopper wagons were acquired. Trains usually comprised twenty hoppers, a brake van, and an engine at front and rear, but when No. 53 was photographed near York Road on 29 August 1967, a minor contretemp had necessitated a half load. When the last spoil train ran, on 2 May 1970, 4½m tons of 'muck' had been moved, the last major freight job tackled by steam in the British Isles.

▼*Plate 119:* Another steam freight service which commenced in the late sixties was on the 3ft. 0in. gauge Isle of Man Railway. All year services ended late in 1965, and it looked as if the line might be abandoned, but it was leased before the 1967 season by the Marquess of Ailsa. The manager, Sir Philip Wombwell, Bt, made valiant efforts to attract freight to the railway, and the bodies were removed from 11 old coaches to provide bogie container flats, one being rebuilt as a bogie well wagon, a rare beast for the NG! The container service ran between Castletown, to which a container freight shipping service had begun, and Douglas. IOMR No. 10, *G H Wood*, of 1905, heads a southbound freight through Santon station on 17 April 1968. Her load comprises an ex MNR 4-w van, the bogie well, three flats and a carriage for braking purposes. The venture proved uneconomic, and narrow gauge container trains ceased a few weeks later. The IOM Railway, Douglas – Port Erin line survives with a seasonal tourist service.

Plate 120: Lacking government millions for dieselisation, industrialists were more cautious in the switch from steam, though new orders were invariably for diesel. One steam user into the 1970s was the Port of Par, lying midway between Plymouth and Truro. Built to serve tin and copper mines, Par latterly handled china clay. As with many early industrial systems, clearances were intended for a horse or small chauldron wagon, and at Par steam had to be shoe-horned into a 7ft. 6in. loading gauge. *Alfred*, a Bagnall 0-4-0ST of 1953 shows how this was done. Most industrial steam has now fallen victim to the diesel, or other handling method, as at Par, which closed in the seventies.

Plate 121: Thus far, the story is familiar, but was BR steam truly dead? In fact, it lived on, not just on the Vale of Rheidol, but in the loco depots now given over to the all conquering diesel or electric, yet few railfans paused to look at the last pre-nationalisation steam on the standard gauge BR. These were the railway steam cranes. RS 1013/50, seen at Rugby in 1964, was one of the most powerful on BR, and one of the last pair of rail cranes built for UK service by Craven Bros in 1930. Costing over £5000, she was a 36 ton crane with relieving bogies and articulated jib foot, but was later upgraded to 50 tons.

LINCOLN CASTLE

▲*Plate 122:* For more than a decade after the fires were dropped for the final time on the last GWR *Castles* in BR ownership, steam powered *Castles* continued in BR passenger service in the North East. These were the paddle steamers *Tattershall Castle, Wingfield Castle* and *Lincoln Castle* built for the Hull – New Holland ferry service of the LNER. *Lincoln Castle* was the last of the trio, and was built by A & J Inglis of Glasgow in 1940. Certified to carry 914 passengers, she was the last example of LNER steam in BR passenger service, when photographed leaving New Holland Pier on 12 July 1974, her sisters having been withdrawn by that time. To re-inforce the message that this is truly BR steam, look at the funnel — the mirror image arrows *are* deliberate, as the normal insignia creates a 'going backwards' impression on the port side of ships.

Plate 123 (Above): Nowadays when the diesel motor vessel has all but eclipsed even the steam turbine from marine use, the days of whirling cranks and motion of the reciprocating steam engine seem remote. A visit to the engine room of the *Lincoln Castle* recalls the enthralling spectacle of a triple expansion compound marine engine, and reminds us that marine engineers, with the greater space of a ship's engine room, compared to a steam locomotive, had solved the problems of using steam not twice, but *three* times. Even then, the turbine, and later the diesel, triumphed. These polished engines drove the 598 ton Lincoln Castle at 10 knots.

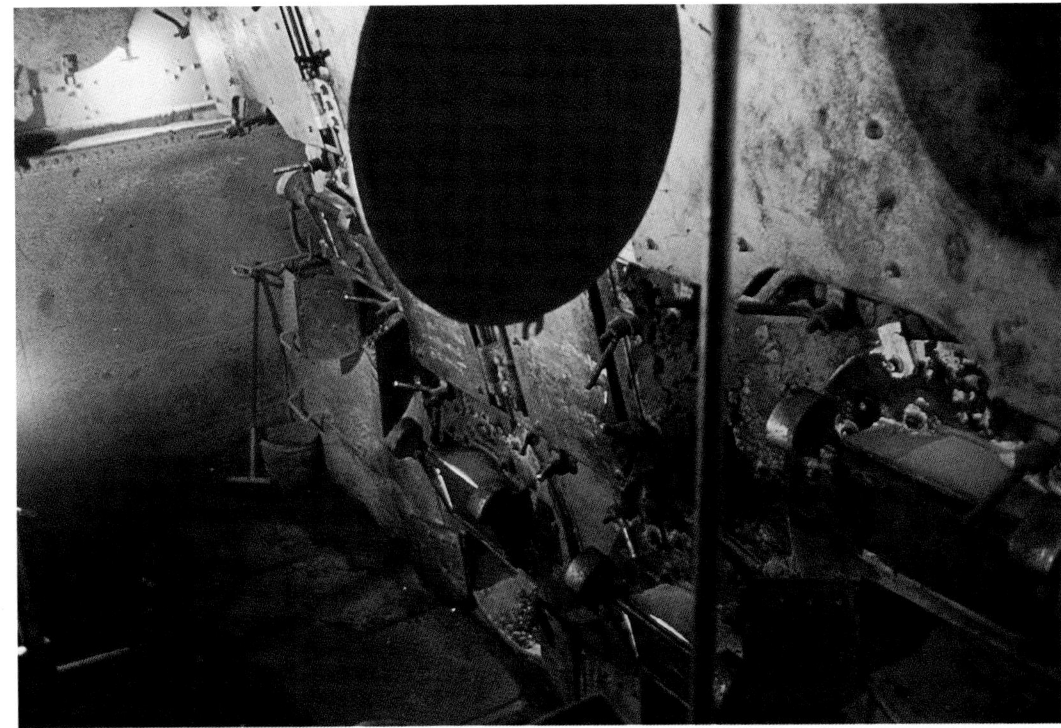

Plate 124 (Right): Many readers will have seen the footplate of a steam locomotive; the stoke hold of a coal fired paddle steamer demanded many of the same skills as were called for from the locomotive fireman. The ruddy glow from the furnaces, and the ship's own lighting, combine to create a pleasing warmth in this glimpse of the business end of steam power. Boiler faults in 1978 precipitated *Lincoln Castle's* withdrawal, for with the imminent opening of the Humber bridge, repair costs could not be justified.

Plate 125: The end of BR standard gauge steam did not write finis to *British* steam, for the UK locomotive builders had been prolific exporters, and as well as providing many of the earliest locomotives for Europe, had supplied Asia, Africa, South America and Australasia into modern times. Thousands of British engines remained in traffic well into the Seventies. Many of the former Colonial lines abounded with operating handicaps, severe gradients, sharp curves and light rail etc. Beyer Peacock produced their first articulated Garratt, in which the boiler is slung between two separate engine units, in 1909. It became one of the export successes of railway history. None were more majestic than the crimson lake liveried Class 59 Beyer-Garratts built for East African Railways in 1955-56. With the collapse of US steam, their 252 ton weight and 83,350lb. tractive effort made them the heaviest and most powerful steam locomotives in the world. To do that on the 3ft. 6in. gauge with a 21 ton axle load was quite something! The MR-influenced livery carried by No. 5921, *Mount Nyiru* at Mombasa, is a reminder that British trained engineers brought the benefits of railways to large parts of the world.

Plate 126: Finale – As the afternoon draws on, and shadows lengthen, a green liveried Stanier Duchess, No. 46230 *Duchess of Buccleuch*, picks her way through the forest of overhead supports at the south end of Crewe station with a Euston express in September 1963, the shadows of the catenary and supports etched across the locomotive and train. It was a prophetic message, not just for No. 46230, which was withdrawn later that year, but for BR steam, for diesel and electric traction had already cast a long shadow. As we leave the *Duchess of Buccleuch* heading her express south towards London and the Setting sun, we reflect that the sun was sinking for British steam after a century and a half.

Index

Note: Locations are indexed where significant, GWR/SR/LMS/LNER/BR appear regularly and are not listed. Other railways are indexed.

Railway Companies/Administrations

Locomotive Classes

GWR

Southern

LMSR

Locomotive Classes (Continued)

LNER

BR

Others

Photography

Chief Mechanical Engineers

Locations

Locations (Continued)

Miscellaneous

PUFFIN BOOKS

Published by the Penguin Group
Penguin Books Ltd, 80 Strand, London WC2R ORL, England
Penguin Group (USA), Inc., 375 Hudson Street, New York, New York 10014, USA
Penguin Books Australia Ltd, 250 Camberwell Road, Camberwell, Victoria 3124, Australia
Penguin Books Canada Ltd, 10 Alcorn Avenue, Toronto, Ontario, Canada M4V 3B2
Penguin Books India (P) Ltd, 11 Community Centre, Panchsheel Park, New Delhi – 110 017, India
Penguin Books (NZ), cnr Airborne and Rosedale Roads, Albany, Auckland 1310, New Zealand
Penguin Books (South Africa) (Pty) Ltd, 24 Sturdee Avenue, Rosebank 2196, South Africa

Penguin Books Ltd, Registered Offices: 80 Strand, London WC2R ORL, England

puffinbooks.com

First published in the USA and Canada by Philomel Books 2002
Published in Great Britain in hardback in Puffin Books 2002
Published in paperback 2005
011

Set in 20pt Gill Sans

Made and printed in China by South China Printing Co. Ltd.

British Library Cataloguing in Publication Data
A CIP catalogue record for this book is available from the British Library

ISBN 978-0-14056-924-7

For Ute and Gerhard

© Mary Lewis
Jane Goodall visiting Eric Carle in his studio.

About the Sloth
by Jane Goodall

Sloths have fascinated me ever since, when I was a child, I learned about their existence in the jungles of South America. There are two species – the three-toed and the two-toed. Sloths can turn their heads about 270 degrees. They can also hang from one leg and rotate their bodies, in a manner most horrifying to observe, through almost 360 degrees. They spend their lives upside down, hanging from the branches. They feed, mostly at dawn and dusk, on shoots and blossoms, leaves and fruits. After feeding for a few hours, moving slowly from one branch to the next, they fall asleep. They sleep fifteen to nineteen hours out of twenty-four, hanging from a branch with their heads laid on their tummies. They look just like a part of the tree because a kind of green algae grows in strange grooves on their long, coarse hairs, so that they become the same greenish colour as their forest world; all kinds of moths and beetles live in their fur. If the sloths are threatened, they defend themselves by striking out with their powerful arms and daggerlike claws. Sloths live in the same tree for days, sometimes weeks. About once a week, looking fat, they climb slowly down to the ground, where they defecate and urinate, carefully bury their waste and climb slowly back – looking slim! When they do move to a new tree, they may have to swim across a river – they are surprisingly fast swimmers. Sloths are silent animals. Occasionally they comment on life with a gentle sigh that sounds like "ah-ee".

When I was a child, sloths, although they were sometimes hunted for food by the indigenous people, had little else to fear. Today they face the destruction of their habitat, as forests are cut down for timber or to create grazing land for cattle. I am so delighted that my friend Eric Carle has chosen to write this book about a sloth. It will do so much to make young people aware of these delightful, gentle, peace-loving creatures. And as more and more people care, so there is greater hope that the sloths, along with their forest world and the other wondrous creatures that live there, will survive.

Eric Carle

“Slowly, Slowly, Slowly,” Said the Sloth

PUFFIN

Slowly,
slowly,
slowly,
a sloth crawled
along a branch of a tree.

Slowly,
slowly,
slowly,
the sloth ate a leaf.

Slowly,
slowly,
slowly,
the sloth fell asleep.

Slowly,
slowly,
slowly,
the sloth woke up.

All day long
the sloth hung
upside down
in the tree.

All night long
the sloth hung
upside down
in the tree.

Even when it rained
the sloth hung
upside down
in the tree.

"Why are you so slow?"
the howler monkey asked one day.

But the sloth didn't answer.

"Why are you so quiet?"
the caiman asked.

But the sloth didn't answer.

"Why are you so boring?"
the anteater asked.

But the sloth didn't answer.

"Tell me," said the jaguar,
"why are you so lazy?"

The sloth thought
and thought
and thought
for a long, long, long time.

Finally, the sloth replied,
"It is true that I am slow, quiet and boring. I am lackadaisical, I dawdle and I dillydally.
I am also unflappable, languid, stoic, impassive, sluggish, lethargic, placid, calm, mellow, laid-back and, well, slothful!
I am relaxed and tranquil, and I like to live in peace.
But I am not lazy."
Then the sloth yawned and said,
"That's just how I am.
I like to do things
slowly,
slowly,
slowly."

Toucan
Armadillo
Postman
Butterfly
Anaconda
Hoatzin
Poison
Dart
Frog
Anteater
Bat
Yellow-spotted
River Turtle
Peccary
Puma
Tapir

Howler Monkey
Cock-of-the-rock
Porcupine
Leaf-cutting Ants
Coati
Macaw
Spider Monkey
Quetzal
Double-crested Basilisk
Jaguar
Caiman
Hummingbird

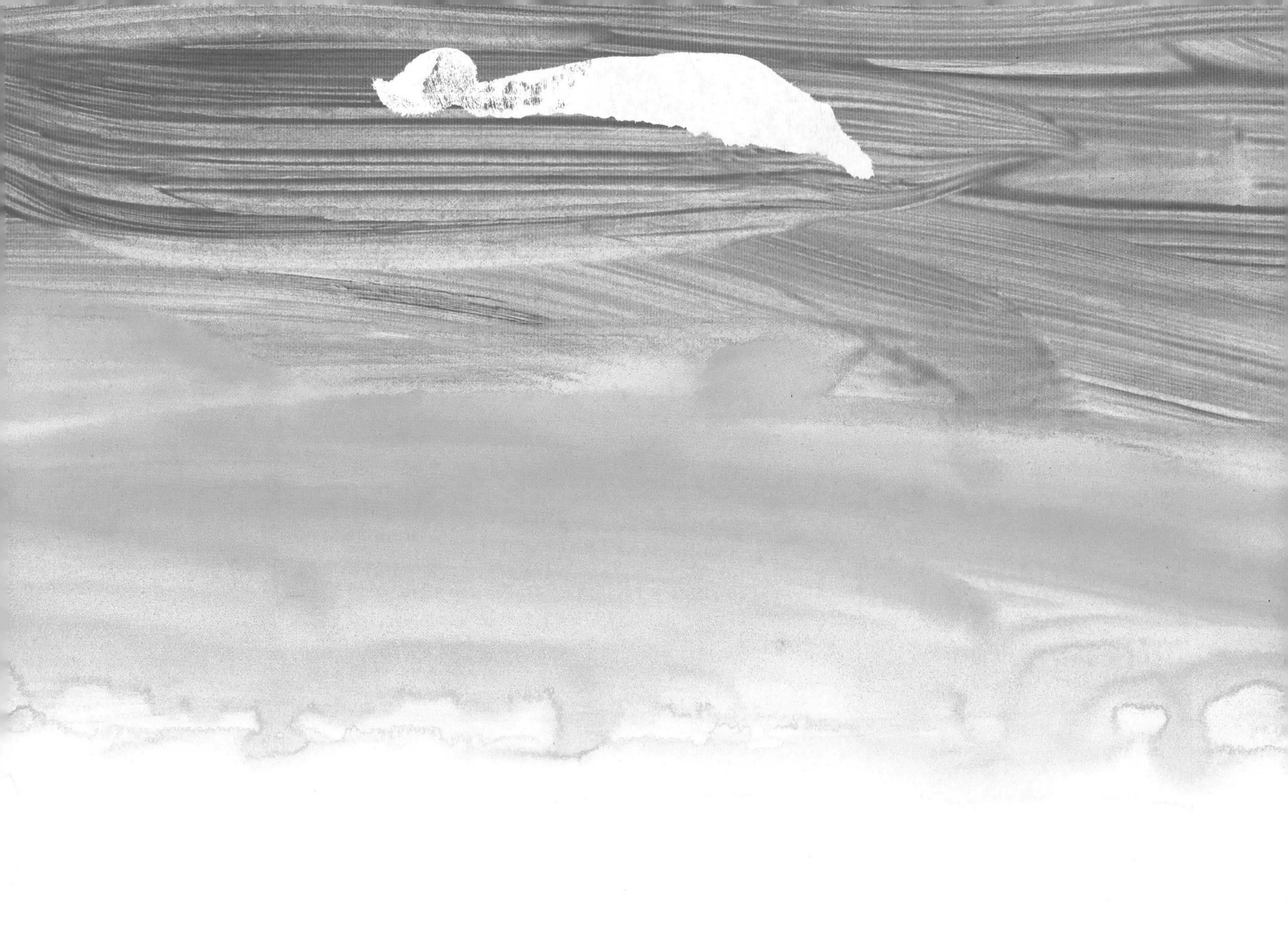